3

A Complete Treatise

Art of Singing: Part One

Da Capo Press Music Reprint Series

MUSIC EDITOR
BEA FRIEDLAND
Ph.D., City University of New York

A Complete Treatise

on the

Art of Singing: Part One

by Manuel Garcia II

First Part, Complete and Unabridged
The Editions of 1841 and 1872
collated, edited and translated by Donald V. Paschke

Da Capo Press • New York • 1984

Library of Congress Cataloging in Publication Data

(Revised for vol. 1, pt. 1)

Garcia, Manuel, 1805-1906.
   École de Garcia. English.
   A complete treatise on the art of singing.

   (Da Capo Press music reprint series)
   Includes bibliographies.
   1. Singing—Methods. I. Paschke, Donald V.
II. Title. III. Series.
MT835.G313   1975   784.9′3   74-23382
ISBN 0-306-76212-9 (v. 1)

This Da Capo Press edition of
A Complete Treatise on the Art of Singing: Part One
is an unabridged translation of the French edition published
in 1841 and 1872, here translated, collated, and edited with
a Preface by Donald V. Paschke.

Published by Da Capo Press, Inc.
A Subsidiary of Plenum Publishing Corporation
233 Spring Street, New York, N.Y. 10013

The School of Garcia

A COMPLETE TREATISE

on

THE ART OF SINGING

by

Manuel Garcia II

First Part

Complete and Unabridged

The editions of 1841 and 1872

collated, edited, and translated by

Donald V. Paschke

TRANSLATOR'S PREFACE

The purposes of this project are: (1) to make available to the vocal profession an English translation of an important work which has been unavailable for many years; and (2) to compare and contrast two editions of that work, the latter of which appeared thirty-one years after the first.

Manuel Garcia is important: first, because of his link to the *bel canto* traditions of Porpora; second, because of the way he combined those traditions with scientific research and with the new style of covered singing introduced into France by the tenor Duprez in 1837; third, because of the consistently high level of artistry and skill attained by his students. It is unlikely that any other teacher of singing has ever produced such an unbroken stream of major vocal artists as that which issued from his studio from the time he began teaching in his father's conservatory in 1829 or 1830 until his death in 1906. That stream was interrupted only by two short periods of military service.

The comparison of the two editions is of interest not so much because of the time lapse and the change of approach to the voice and its development which several years of experience often brings, but rather because of the fact that in the intervening years Garcia had invented the laryngoscope and was thus the first person able to study the living larynx during the act of phonation. It is apparent from perusing the two editions of his method that his use of the laryngeal mirror in most instances verified the theories which the author had formed earlier as a result of both his knowledge of the anatomy of the vocal mechanism and his experience as a teacher.

The author, Manuel Patricio Rodriguez Garcia (1805-1906), was the son of Manuel del Popolo Vicente Rodriguez (1775-1832), a noted Spanish tenor and composer who adopted the name Garcia as a stage name, later making it his legal surname. The father was born and received his first musical training in Seville. He had established himself as a tenor of the top rank in both Spain and France even before going to Naples in 1812 to learn the Porpora method under Giovanni Ansani. Ansani may have studied under Porpora himself, having been in his twentieth year when Porpora died in 1768. Rossini composed the role of Count Almaviva in *The Barber of Seville* for the elder Manuel, and the opera was premiered on February 5, 1816. Only a few weeks later the family left Naples to settle again in Paris. From there, they branched out to conquer not only London, but also the New World. After long sojourns in New York City and Mexico City, the troupe returned to France where the elder Garcia soon retired from the stage to devote his full time to teaching. He had already engaged himself in that activity for a number of years, having taught his wife to sing, as well as his three children. The famous tenor Adolph Nourrit also was his student.

Manuel Patricio was born on March 17, 1805, in Zafra, Spain. He was left in the care of his grandparents in Madrid from the time his parents left for France in late 1807 until they sent for him from Naples in 1814. After his arrival there he was given some occasional informal lessons by his father's teacher, Ansani. M. Sterling MacKinlay,

Garcia's biographer, conjectures that if Ansani indeed had his early lessons from Porpora himself, the later students of Garcia who lived into the twentieth century could say that their teacher had his early lessons from a man whose teacher was born within two or three years of the birth of Bach and Handel. (a Perhaps no more direct connection to the first golden age of *bel canto* exists in our own time than this one, even if Ansani was a second-generation student of Porpora. The bulk of Manuel's lessons, however, were under his father and Zingarelli. Those lessons from his father can safely be assumed to be extensions of the lessons from Ansani.

Manuel's training continued in Paris, and in late 1825 the family traveled to New York to introduce Italian grand opera to the New World. The younger Manuel's debut was in the role of Figaro in *The Barber of Seville*. It took place in New York on November 29, 1825. The company for that New York season included the father as the *primo tenore*, the mother and Mme Barbiere as the sopranos, Maria Garcia, the seventeen-year-old sister of the author, as the only alto, young Manuel as the only baritone, Giovanni Crivelli as the *secondo tenore*, d'Angrisani as the *basso cantante*, and Rosich as the *buffo caricato*. The chorus was recruited from choir singers in New York. After a season extending until the end of the following September, the company departed for Mexico City, where the younger Manuel often substituted for his ailing father on the tenor roles. Although the highest passages were revised

---

a) M. Sterling MacKinlay, *Garcia the Centenarian and His Times* (New York: D. Appleton and Company, 1908), p. 26.

downward, the high tessituras apparently did irreparable damage to the younger man's voice, and he was obliged to return to France to prepare to go to Naples for further study as his parents still had their hearts set on an operatic career for him.

His sister Maria did not accompany her family's company to Mexico because of her sudden marriage in New York to a French merchant, François-Eugène Malibran. After the failure of that marriage, Maria left New York and arrived in Paris at nearly the same time as Manuel. Manuel postponed his departure for Naples for about three months while he helped Maria prepare for her Paris debut. His sister thus became his first famous student.

When he went to Naples to continue his own studies, Manuel seems to have made some additional mistakes in judgement, such as trying to mimic the huge bass tones of the great basso, Luigi Lablache, whom he cites in different places in his method as the example of his subject matter. MacKinlay states that apparently further damage was done to the already weakened voice by such attempts, and when he finally made his Italian debut, the critical reviews confirmed his suspicions that the operatic stage was not for him. (b He returned to Paris to prepare for another career.

Strangely, that career was not the teaching of singing, but rather, he studied navigation and astronomy and actually obtained a post on a ship. However, before he set sail, he was dissuaded by his mother

---

b) *Ibid.*, p. 90.

and sisters. He began his full time teaching career in his father's
conservatory as his father's assistant, for by that time his parents had
returned from Mexico.

But his father's domineering ways did not fit Manuel's spirit at
that time, so Manuel left his father's home and employ to join the
quartermaster corps of the French army during the invasion of Algeria in
1830. Upon his return from North Africa late that year, he was attached
to military hospitals where he had the opportunity to study in detail
the anatomy of the vocal mechanism, a knowledge which served as the
basis for his theories of phonation and control of the voice.

We noted above that Manuel's sister Maria (1808-1836) was his
first pupil. She had made her operatic debut in London under their
father's tutelage before the voyage to New York. After their father's
death in 1832, Manuel became her only teacher. She was acknowledged as
the unrivaled contralto of her era and became a legend in her own life-
time, in spite of the fact that she died at the young age of twenty-
eight of complications following a fall from a horse.

Pauline Garcia (1821-1910)--who sang most of her career under her
married name of Viardot--was Manuel's younger sister, having been born
when he was sixteen. Her father began developing her voice gradually
from the time she was four, but since she was only eleven years old when
her father died, the guidance of her voice during its all-important
maturing years fell to her brother. As was the case with the other
members of her family, general musicianship was regarded as being
extremely important, and she was given lessons in piano by the young

Franz Liszt, and in composition by Reicha. Her voice was not nearly so great as that of her sister Maria, but, as Manuel himself was often heard to say, she sang with so much intelligence that her listeners were unaware of the lack of native beauty in the instrument. Her performing career lasted twenty-five years, and she retired to teach, first at Baden-Baden, where she became a close friend of Brahms, and later in Paris. Like her brother, she had a long teaching career which lasted practically to the time of her death at the age of eighty-nine.

A list of Manuel's other star pupils, besides his two sisters, would make up much of a "Who's Who in Singing" for the final seven decades of the nineteenth century, as well as the beginning of the twentieth century. He moved from Paris to London in 1848 and taught at the Royal Academy of Music until his retirement in 1895 at the age of ninety. After that he taught at his home until very shortly before his death on July 1, 1906, at the age of 101 years. His most distinguished pupil was undoubtedly Jenny Lind. Among the others were Mathilde Marchesi, who became a very famous teacher in her own right, Julius Stockhausen, one of Germany's greatest singers and teachers, and Sir Charles Santley in England. Richard Wagner sent his neice Johanna to him in 1845, and many years later invited him to train the singers for the first Beyreuth Festival, an honor which Garcia declined because of his heavy schedule in London.

Garcia's first major work as an author seems to have been his *Mémoire sur la voix humaine*, submitted to the French Academy of Sciences in November, 1840. It was a description of his theories of the formation of the registers and the timbres of the singing voice, as well as of the various applications of them to the different voice classifications. It was reported upon and accepted only after the investigating committee called upon Garcia to demonstrate his theories with his students. The *Mémoire* then served as a basis for his *Traité complet sur l'Art du Chant*, Part One of which appeared in 1841. In Part One the author presents the means of developing a vocal instrument which is adequate to perform the music of his day.

In Part Two, which appeared in 1847 (our translation, collation, and edition of Part Two was published in 1975), Garcia discusses the interpretation of song, or the application of all the various techniques presented in Part One. Part Two presents a very comprehensive view of the vocal performance practices of the mid-nineteenth century. It is copiously illustrated with musical examples to make the exposition especially lucid.

After his invention of the laryngoscope in 1854, Garcia wrote an exposition of his observations with that instrument under the title: *Physiological observations of the human voice*, which was submitted to the Royal Academy in 1855, and was published in their *Proceedings*. The following year he published his *Nouveau Traité Sommaire sur l'Art du Chant*, which was essentially his original method with most revisions taking the form of omissions rather than alterations. It is a reprint of that 1856 edition, dated 1872 and referred to by Garcia in the preface as the sixth edition of his method, which we have used to compare the earlier and later forms of the method.

In 1894, in order to reply to some attacks on his method, especially his use of the *coup de glotte* as a training device, he published his *Hints on Singing*, with the sole purpose of clarifying some of the questions that had arisen regarding his earlier publications.

Garcia's later writings seem to have been translated into English, but not his earlier ones. We have included the preface to the 1841 Schott edition of Part One, which contains a lengthy extract from the *Mémoire*, as part of this project. We do not know how much more there was to the *Mémoire*, and we have found no other translation of that work. Although there is an English edition of both parts of the *Nouveau Traité* (Part One of which was published in the United States, unsigned and undated, by Oliver Ditson), no English versions of either Part One or Part Two in their earliest editions (1841-1851) were discovered. Both of these printings were slightly abridged from the French. In addition, Albert Garcia (1875-1946), Manuel's grandson, published in 1924 *Garcia's Treatise on the Art of Singing*, described as "a compendious method of instruction." (c   An examination of this edition revealed that it is a further abridgement of the English version mentioned above.

The *Physiological observations on the human voice* was written in English (his only work in our language) and was reprinted in the *Laryngoscope* magazine on the occasion of Garcia's hundredth birthday, which happened to coincide with the fiftieth anniversary of its publication. It was immediately translated into French and published in France. The

---

c) Manuel Garcia, *Garcia's Treatise on the Art of Singing*, ed. Albert Garcia (London: Leonard and Company, 1924).

Hints on Singing was written in French, but was initially published in English in a translation by Garcia's second wife, Beata. (d A second edition (still in print) was edited slightly by Garcia's former student, Hermann Klein. (e

In order to make the reader aware of portions of Part One which do not appear in the later edition, we have enclosed those portions, whether they are regular text material, musical examples or exercises, or footnotes, between single asterisks. Portions which appear in the 1872 edition, but not in the 1841 edition, are enclosed between double asterisks. Places where actual differences in wording, placement of sentences or paragraphs, different musical examples or exercises, etc., occur are marked with capital letters in boxes, and these are explained in corresponding places in the Appendix.

Unlike our policy in Part Two, where all the translator footnotes were gathered into a separate appendix, such footnotes in Part One are placed at the bottom of the same page as the citation. They are marked by the beginning of a parenthesis followed by a lower case letter.

As we did in Part Two, we placed French words with more than one possible meaning in brackets after our translation of that word. Subject headings which are given in different languages by the author are

---

d) Manuel Garcia, *Hints on Singing*, tr. Beata Garcia (London: Ascherberg, Hopwood and Crew; New York: E. Schuberth, c. 1894). MacKinlay states that the actual publication date was in early 1895, *op. cit.*, p. 261.

e) Manuel Garcia, *Hints on Singing*, newly ed. and rev. by Hermann Klein (London: Ascherberg, Hopwood and Crew, 1911).

presented in parentheses in this printing. Optional translations of subject headings supplied by the translator or original headings by the author which may be translated in more than one way are given in brackets. The reader may thus form his or her own conclusions, should some ambiguity still exist in our English rendering of those terms.

The translator felt very strongly that the vocal exercises must be planned so they could be read without the inconvenience of turning pages. In order to attain that aim and still make them legible, he undertook the task of writing out all the exercises by hand. It is hoped that the additional convenience and legibility will sufficiently reward the many hours that task required.

The translator wishes to acknowledge several valuable contributions: first, the encouragement of Dr. Berton Coffin, his mentor at the University of Colorado; second, the use of the copy of the 1872 edition owned by the Norlin Library of the University of Colorado; third, the diligent and valuable service of proofreading by Dr. James Penrod of the Eastern New Mexico University Department of Languages and Literature, Mr. Mark Todd of Clovis, New Mexico, a graduate of that same department, and Mr. Lewis Toland of Portales, New Mexico, an Eastern New Mexico University graduate with degrees in business and religion.

Finally, there was a special quality of encouragement and prodding which was especially valuable whenever it seemed this project was getting bogged down or set aside due to the press of more prosaic daily routine. Because of that constant encouragement, this volume is dedicated to its source, the translator's wife, Helen, with fond affection.

TABLE OF CONTENTS

Chapter

PREFACE TO THE FIRST EDITION

It would be curious to know the progress which the art of singing has followed from the most remote times to our own day. One would wish especially to be able to study in detail the teaching practiced in the 17th and 18th centuries, in the schools, so prolific in brilliant results, of Fedi, Pistocchi, Porpora, Bernacchi, Egizio, etc.[1]

Unfortunately, that epoch has left to us only some vague and incomplete documents of its traditions. The works of Tosi, Mancini, Herbst, Agricola, some scattered passages in the histories of Bontempi, Burney, Hawkins, and Baini, give us only an approximate and confused idea of the methods then followed.

The son of an artist generally appreciated as a singer, and who is recommended as a master by the merited reputations of several of his students,[2] I have collected his instructions, fruits of a long experience and of a most cultivated musical taste.

It is his method which I have wanted to reproduce by trying to reduce it to a more theoretical form and by attaching the results to the causes.

As all the effects of singing are, in the final analysis, the product of the vocal organ, I have submitted the study of it to physiological considerations. This procedure has enabled me to recognize the

---

[1]From these schools came the illustrious singers Ferri, Pasi, Farinelli, Raff, Gizziello, etc.

[2]Maria Malibran, Adolphe Nourrit, etc.

precise number of registers and the true range of each of them; I have been able to determine the fundamental timbres of the voice, their mechanism and their distinctive characteristics, the various methods of performing passages, the nature and the mechanism of the trill, etc.

This manner of considering the teaching [of singing] can, I believe, make it, as a whole, more precise and more complete. All the effects of singing, whether they belong to one particular execution of the melody, or they depend upon some special timbre imparted to the voice by the emotion, can be analyzed and conveyed in a perceptible form.

In order to apply the theory thus conceived in a rational manner, one should, in our opinion, isolate the difficulties and make each of them the object of a special labor. The exercises appropriate to form and to develop the voice are indicated in the first part of this work. In the second, I will approach the application of this first study to pronunciation, to the art of phrasing, to the color of the emotions in the different styles, etc.

Perhaps one was expecting to encounter some vocalises in this work; the custom, we know, is at the same time very old and almost general today. If, however, we have excluded them from this method, it is because they no longer have, for us, the advantage that they formerly presented, and that they bring along some inconveniences which the old methods knew how to prevent.[3]

---

[3]This fact is connected with some curious details of musical

Vocalises are melodies without words, offering the student the combination of all the difficulties in singing. This study supposes that the student already knows how to place the voice, to make it pure, equal, intense, to blend the registers, to vary its timbres, to control the emission of the air, to perform scales, arpeggios, trills, mordents, in a word, that he possesses all the resources of the singer, with one single exception, pronunciation. All these particular difficulties, combined in vocalises, annoy and hold back the student for a long time. It is true that he can persist in all these details which impede him separately, but each of these details is connected to a group of

---

history. In the 16th, 17th, and 18th centuries, one would study music only with the aid of the voice. The students specially destined for singing were directed in that study by the same master who had taught them solfege. Sometimes, in order to avoid the difficulties which were then in force, one would replace the names of the notes with a vowel. From this accidentally employed procedure was born the custom, today so common, of teaching indistinctly, by the vocalise, both music [reading] and the specific song. The present system seems, at the first approach, to be only the continuation of the old system, and yet the application of it is essentially different. Formerly, in the teaching of solfege (*la solmisation*), the master, by careful precautions, would prevent in advance all the faulty habits which might have been able to prejudice the future studies of the singer. He watched him in the emission of the voice, in the articulation of the names of the notes, in the manner of breathing; he habituated him to a correct and pure feeling for the music, etc. Later, one approached, by means of special and vocalized exercises, the complete development of the resources of the voice. One had recourse to the *messa di voce*, the *portamento*, the *trill*, the *groppolo*, the *diminutioni*, etc. Today the study of music and that of singing are no longer confided to the same master, and the first of these studies is only the incomplete or faulty preparation for the second. Moreover, the difficulties of the old nomenclature having completely disappeared, nothing prevents us henceforth from omitting the name of each note, and of thus depriving ourselves of the most effective means of teaching music reading. Finally, the vocalise, used as the only exercise for the study of the material difficulties of singing, presents some difficulties which we are developing here.

difficulties of the same nature which should have been, earlier and by itself, the object of a special study. The trill, for example, in place of being studied in a particular phrase, should be studied first alone and in all its various forms. This labor would surely prepare one for the application of it to all the passages in which it would appear. There would be an economy of time to begin thus, and one would attain more extensive and more complete results.

Such are the motives which have caused us to prefer the analytical method to the contrary system more generally adopted.

PREFACE TO THE SIXTH EDITION
PRELIMINARY NOTICE

The study of the mechanism of the human voice, very instructive for the physiologist, can also have some undeniable advantages for the singer. Nothing, in fact, can be more valuable to him than to know by what procedures the vocal instrument manages to produce the vibrations, to what operation of the organs we owe the range of the voice, the registers, the timbres, the ring of the tones, their intensity, their volume, the rapid succession of the notes, etc. If he could obtain that knowledge, the singer would find in it the secret of the proper means of smoothing the difficulties which hamper his studies; he also could more surely avoid the dangers which cause the voice to be improperly used or subject it to abuse.

Until our days the physiologist possessed only some approximate notions, obtained by induction, of this part of science. In order to make them precise he lacked a means of direct observation. This means

has been furnished to him recently by the *laryngoscope*; he can today, by

carrying his look into the interior of the larynx, examine it while the

voice is being produced, and, connecting the movements which he sees

there to his knowledge of anatomy, establish his theories on well veri-

fied facts.

The laryngoscope is a small apparatus of my own invention with

which I have been able to be the first to examine the interior of the

larynx during the act of singing.

Since my observations have been published,[4] the instruments which

I used have become, in the hands of doctors, an important means of diag-

nosis.

These instruments, which I believe useful to make known to pupils

who are destined to the art of singing, consist of two mirrors. One of

them, very small, is fixed at the end of a long stem and is placed

against the uvula at the top of the throat, the reflecting face turned

downward. One should warm it moderately at the moment of use in order

that the breath may not cloud it. The other, a hand mirror, is meant to

direct on the first a ray of light which permits it to illuminate the

---

[4]See: *Observations on the human voice*; received March 22, 1855.
In the *Proceedings of the Royal Society*, London, vol. VII, no. 13, pp.
399-410, 1855. Translated into French under the title of: *Observations
physiologiques sur la voix humaine*, Paris, imp. de Duverger, 1855, in 8°
of 16 pages. Second edition, preceded by a *Notice on the Invention of
the Laryngoscope*, by P. Richard, Paris, Asselin, 1861, in 8°. *Etude
pratique sur le Laryngoscope*, by Dr. Edouard Fournié, memoire read to
the *Académie des sciences*, November 10, 1862, Paris, Ad. Delahaye, 1863,
in 8°.

glottis and to raise the image of it to the eye of the observer. The

first mirror is flat, squared at blunt angles; it is about eight milli-

meters [*sic*: this is surely a misprint in the 1872 edition; *eighteen*

millimeters would be a more likely size] long on each side and is sold-

ered to a stem twelve to fourteen centimeters long at an angle of 110°

to 145°. This bending is required by the vaulted form of the pharyngeal

region. The reflector mirror can be flat or concave.

These mirrors have been submitted, in the applications which

doctors have made of them, to various arrangements, of which the designs

shown here represent some cases.[5] These illustrations will perhaps give

a more exact idea of the laryngoscope than rather long explanations

would do.

Fig. 1. The hand mirror directs
the single ray against the little
guttural mirror and receives the
image of the glottis from it.

Fig. 2. Here the light is
reflected from the concave
mirror onto the laryngeal or
pharyngeal (guttural) mirror,
and from that onto the little
flat mirror where the image
of the glottis shows to the
observer.

---

[5]We owe the arrangements illustrated in figures 2, 3, 4, and 5 to
doctors Turck, Czermak, Ed. Fournié, and George Johnson.

Fig. 3. The light is received first by the concave forehead mirror, then reflected onto the hand mirror, and from that to the guttural mirror.

Fig. 4. The observer sees the image of the glottis in the flat mirror immediately above the round hole through which the light which illuminates the laryngeal mirror passes.

Fig. 5. The light received by the forehead mirror is returned to the guttural mirror where the image of the glottis appears.

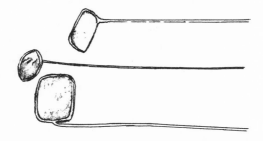

Fig. 6. Laryngeal mirrors, one third size.

The flame of the lamp can, in each case, be encircled with a paper reflector.

The forehead mirror (*l'Ophthalmoscope de ruete*) is concave and is eight to ten centimeters in diameter, with a focal length of twenty to thirty centimeters. It is attached to the forehead by a headband on which it is hinged in every direction by means of a ball-and-socket pivot.

The practical advantages assured to the singer by the result of this examination were presented in the edition of my method which appeared in 1856. That edition is reproduced exactly in this one which I offer today to the public as the sixth edition of the work.

REPORT

on the

MEMOIRE ON THE HUMAN VOICE

Presented to the Academy of Sciences

by

Mr. MANUEL GARCIA

(Commissioners: Messers Magendie, Savary, Dutrochet, Reporter.)
(Extracted from the minutes of the sessions of the Academy of Sciences,
meeting of April 12, 1841.)

The Academy has charged us, Messers Magendie, Savary, and myself,
to make a report to it on a memoir which has been presented to it by Mr.
Manuel Garcia, and which is entitled, *Memoire on the Human Voice*. The
state of health of Mr. Savary has not permitted him to join the Commis-
sion; another colleague, of whom we have to deplore the recent loss, Mr.
Savart, to whom acoustics owes so much original research, had also been
added to us; he was, as we were, witness to the facts which we are going
to have the honor of communicating to the Academy.

The theory of the formation and the variation of sounds by the
human vocal organ is far from being complete; people are not even in
accord as to the kind of instrument to which the human vocal organ
should be compared. Nearly all physicists have considered it as being
of the gender of wind instruments in which the sounds are engendered by

the vibrations of certain solid and elastic bodies. Mr. Savart, on the contrary, has compared the vocal organ to one of those instruments used by hunters to imitate the singing of certain birds, an instrument of the flute type in which the sound is engendered exclusively by the vibrations of the air which knocks against the walls of a cavity or which breaks on the edge of a bevel.

In spite of the authority which our colleague necessarily had in acoustical matters, it is very necessary to say that his theory on the voice recruited few partisans; also, he was telling us himself a few days before his death that he was going to modify it and complete it. Let us hope that there will be found among his papers some traces of this work, which cannot fail to be of great interest.

However that may be, the vocal organ is so perfect, it has results so marvellous and so diverse, that one would be tempted to believe that it is not at all a single instrument and that it enjoys the admirable privilege of transforming itself incessantly into a multitude of different instruments. You see it function, for example, in the chest voice; you see it doing something in the falsetto voice; would one not say that these two kinds of registers are produced by two instruments which are substituted one for the other? There has been, however, no success as yet in determining what is the difference which exists, without doubt, in the mechanism of the production of these two kinds of voice, whose qualities offer such deep differences. Yet one has gained the certitude that they are perfectly distinct and that they are not at all the immediate continuation of each other. In fact, in the vicinity

of the point of junction of these two voices or *registers*, there where
the lowest notes of the falsetto voice give way to the highest notes of
the full voice, there are several of these notes which one can produce
equally by using each of these two voices. This fact, known by the artists, has been introduced to physiological science only a small number
of years ago. One finds it set forth for the first time in the work of
doctor Rusch, entitled: *Philosophie de la voix humaine*, a work of which
a part has been translated from English into French by doctor Bennati.
"It must not be imagined," says Rusch, *"that the scale particular to
that mode of voice* (the falsetto) *is comprised between the last note of
the natural voice* (the chest voice) *and the highest note which one can
perform. One can still form a kind of falsetto a little below the point
which ties the natural voice to this kind of intonation."* The facts
which have been submitted to us by Mr. Manuel Garcia have fully confirmed this assertion. That able professor of singing has trained some
students to whom he has taught the art of maneuvering their vocal organs
with enough facility to separate clearly and at will the sounds which
derive from the full voice and those which derive from the falsetto
voice. Thus we have heard some voices of men and some of women, after
having followed to their upper limit the sounds which belong to the full
voice, take the falsetto voice in order to rise higher, then descend
diatonically, keeping the falsetto, down to a certain distance below the
limit at which the full voice had stopped, in such a manner that the
sounds produced by the two voices were compared. The range of the portion common to the two voices or *registers* of the chest and the falsetto

is variable according to the individuals and according to the technique [*l'habitude*] which makes the optional usage of one or the other of these two registers in the *medium* of the voice more or less easy for them. Most commonly that range is from a sixth to an octave, and it sometimes extends to a tenth. According to Mr. Garcia, that part which is common to the two registers is placed on the same notes for the man's voice and the woman's voice.

There is no doubt, according to these facts, that the full voice, or chest voice, and the falsetto voice, are produced by a particular and important modification of the mechanism of the vocal instrument. This conclusion is also confirmed by an observation of Mr. Garcia, an observation which particularly struck our colleague, Mr. Savart, who was a witness to it as we were. The full voice and the falsetto voice, in order to produce the same note in the range which is common to them, use a quantity of air which is not at all, by far, the same. This is what Mr. Garcia demonstrated to us by the following experiment. A singer having his chest as filled with air as it could be, produced, with the full voice, a determined note, taken in the part common to the two registers, and he sustained this vocal sound until the air contained in his lungs was exhausted. The pendulum of a metronome served by its oscillations to indicate the time during which that vocal sound lasted; then, having refilled his lungs with air, the singer produced the same note with the falsetto voice, and he sustained it as long as that was possible for him. Now we saw, in these two experiments repeated several times, that the pendulum offered twenty-four to twenty-six oscillations during the length of the full voice sound, while it offered only sixteen to eighteen oscillations during the length of the same sound in the falsetto voice.

This experiment proves that, in a given time, and for the production of the same diatonic tone, the vocal instrument spends more air while producing the falsetto voice than while producing the full or chest voice.

According to the common opinion of artists, the falsetto voice forms a particular register which differs both from that of the chest, which is lower, and from the register of the *head voice*, which is higher. Mr. Garcia does not at all concur in this opinion; he considers the falsetto voice and the head voice as belonging to one and the same register, offering, in all its range, the same mechanism for the production of the tones. He bases his opinion on this sure consideration: that the falsetto voice and the head voice offer a perfect and constant continuity; there are no marginal [*limitrophes*] sounds which can be produced alternately by one or the other of these two voices, as was just seen relative to the transiton between the chest voice and the falsetto voice. This last voice and the head voice would then indeed belong to one and the same register, which Mr. Garcia designates under the name of the *falsetto-head* register.

It is generally known that when the human voice rises from low to high, as much in the chest voice as in the *falsetto-head* voice, the larynx gradually rises. This gradual ascension of the larynx has been considered influential on the progressive increase of the highness of the sounds, in that this ascension operates the progressive shortening of the vocal tube. Some physiologists have doubted that this shortening of the vocal tube might have the influence in the degree of highness of the vocal sounds which was thus attributed to it. We do not have to concern ourselves here at all with these theoretical questions; our task is simply to relate some facts, and here the art of singing presents us with some new ones. Here is what they consist of:

The full voice and the falsetto voice, each while keeping its own particular mode of production, can offer two principle varieties in their timbre, varieties which Mr. Garcia designates under the names of *clear timbre* and *sombre timbre*. These two timbres of the voice are ordinarily designated by the artists, the first under the name of *white voice* [*voix blanche*] and the second under the name of *darkened voice* [*voix sombrée*]. Now, in the production of the chest or *falsetto-head* voice, whether with the *clear timbre* or with the *sombre timbre*, there is manifested in the position of the larynx and in that of the velum some very noticeable changes. Here are the facts of which Mr. Garcia has given us witness.

In the diatonic production of the tones from low to high, as much so with the full or chest voice as with the *falsetto-head*, and with the *clear timbre*, one observes a continual and gradual ascension of the larynx; the velum is then constantly lowered. It is not the same when the voice passes to the *sombre timbre*.

In the full or chest voice produced with the *sombre timbre*, and while rising from the lowest tones to the highest tones which are appropriate to it, the larynx remains constantly fixed in its lowest position, and the velum is lifted. It is the same in the production of the *sombre timbre* in the lowest part of the falsetto voice, or that part in which the tones can be produced equally with the full voice; but when the singer passes, still in *sombre timbre*, to the highest part of the falsetto voice, to that which is designated by the artists under the name of *head voice*, then the larynx rises a little, but much less than it does when this same head voice is produced with the *clear timbre*. In order to make this difference heard to your Commissioners, some students of Mr. Garcia, well trained in imparting at will to their voices the *clear timbre* or the *sombre timbre*, made us hear, in falsetto voice, some scales in which each note was given alternately in *clear timbre* and *sombre timbre*. One then perfectly distinguished the difference between these two timbres, the one brilliant and the other a little dull; and although it was the same note of the falsetto voice which was heard, we saw the larynx fixed in a high position for the production of that note in the *clear timbre*, and then descend considerably for the production of that note in *sombre timbre*; we could follow with the eye and with the finger that alternating ascent and descent of the larynx.

These observations are not at all completely new for the physiology of the voice.

In fact, they were presented to the Academy of Sciences, June 1, 1840,[6] by Messers Diday and Petrequin, in a memoir which has as its

---

[6]The *Mémoire* of Mr. Garcia was presented to the Academy of Sciences only on November 16, 1840.

objective the physiological study of the darkened voice [*voix sombrée*], an unusual voice which was then known for only three years in France, where it had been imported from Italy by a famous artist attached to our first lyric stage. In this memoir is recorded the physiological fact of the lowered and fixed position of the larynx in the diatonic production of all the sounds of the chest voice in the *voix sombrée*, but these authors did not follow at all the same sombre timbre in the phenomenae which it presents when it invests the falsetto voice with its unique character. They even appear to have thought that this sombre timbre could only affect the chest voice. Mr. Garcia can therefore claim a part in the observation of the mechanism which presides in the formation of the *voix sombrée*.[7] This mechanism shows that with the full or chest voice, as with the falsetto or head voice, the human vocal organ can give the same scales with very different lengths of the vocal tube, which [changes of length] merely bring about changes in the timbre of the voice. It follows from this that the different lengths of the vocal tube do not necessarily have the effects on the determination of [the pitch of] the tone which have been attributed to them, and that these same differences in the lengths of the vocal tube are constantly in accord with the existence of the clear timbre or the sombre timbre of the voice.

Beyond the two principal timbres designated under the names of

----

[7]In a letter which was read to the Academy of Sciences April 19, 1841, Mr. Garcia established that the lowered and fixed position of the larynx has been known to him since 1832, and that since that time he has not stopped propagating that fact by teaching it to all his students.

clear timbre and *sombre timbre*, there are several other secondary ones. Such are, for example, the *guttural timbre*, the *nasal timbre*, etc. Mr. Garcia tries to determine the mechanical conditions of these timbres; we will say nothing in that regard, not having verified at all the assertions of Mr. Garcia.

There sometimes exists in the human voice a lower register for the deepest [*la gravite*] tones, notes which are lower than those which can be given in the chest voice by basso-profundos. This register, called the *contra-bass* register by Mr. Garcia, has as yet been observed in its full development only in some singers used in Russia for religious singing. It is doctor Bennati who first called it to the attention of the physiologists. The sounds of this register indubitably belong to a vocal instrument *sui generis*, very different from that to which the sounds of the chest register are due. In the lowest sounds of this latter voice, or register, the larynx lowers below the position of rest; in the very deepest tones of the contra-bass register, the larynx, on the contrary, is lifted to its highest possible elevation. Mr. Garcia was able to show us, in this register, only a very deep and very raucous tone which resembled the growling of an animal rather than the tone of a human voice. But one of us was able to study, in the Russian singer Yvanoff, the contra-bass voice which that artist possesses, and which descends as far as the GG an octave below that of ordinary basses. Although that note was infinitely superior in tone, or rather in noise, to that which Mr. Garcia showed us, it would be difficult to include it in singing.

One easily understands from this account that one and the same mechanism could not account for the formation of all the musical sounds which the human vocal organ can produce. That organ can truly be considered as being capable, by itself, of representing a collection of instruments, all different from each other, marvelous modifications which occur and establish themselves with an admirable dispatch, according to the will of the trained singer. If then, ceasing to consider the vocal organ as a musical instrument, we enter into the consideration of all the non-musical sounds which that organ can produce, through the variety of the sounds of words, through the imitation of certain sounds or the cries of certain animals, etc., one could only be profoundly astonished by the multiplicity of changes to which that organ, which appears so simple in structure, is susceptible.

In short, we think that Mr. Garcia, by his sagacity and the exactness of his studies as a professor of singing, has observed and described in his *Mémoire* several interesting facts, of which it will be necessary henceforth to take account in the physical theory of the human voice. We have the honor of proposing that the Academy express to him its satisfaction.

The conclusions of this Report have been adopted.

AN ABBREVIATED DESCRIPTION
OF THE VOCAL APPARATUS [A]

We believe it our duty to place at the beginning of this method an abbreviated description of the vocal apparatus. It seems to us impossible to understand the mechanism of an instrument well if one does not first have some notion of the different parts which compose it.

This anatomical statement is addressed, not to physiologists, but to singers. Also, let us borrow from science only the details strictly necessary for the intelligence of our theories, and some technical expressions, so it will be necessary to accept them just as anatomy presents them. Let our readers be not at all frightened by them; these few terms will easily become familiar to them and cannot be the occasion of a real difficulty.

The vocal apparatus, rather complex on the whole, is under the immediate subjection of the respiratory apparatus, and these two functions, the respiration and the voice, are intimately tied to each other and belong to a common ensemble of organs. Thus, for a tone to be produced, it is necessary that the breath first have been accumulated in the chest, and it is when it is driven from there that, as a consequence of a reciprocal action between it and certain parts of the tube through which it travels, the voice is formed. We are going to describe the vocal organs by following the path which the air follows during the phenomenon of expiration.

It is necessary to consider first the two lungs, imminently

elastic spongy masses, which occupy both sides of the chest and follow its movements. The essential organs of respiration, the lungs perform the functions of an organ bellows which furnishes the air necessary for the sonorous vibrations. The lungs, in order to receive outside air, need for the walls of the chest, by moving apart, to provide space where they can dilate freely. With this increase in capacity is combined the lowering of the diaphragm, a large and complex muscle [which rises] from the sides of the chest, which serves as its base and separates it from the abdomen. The air penetrates the lungs and leaves them by a multitude of tubes called *bronchi* which, disposed in the manner of tree branches, are very fine at their beginning, then increase in volume by combining, and finally, end by forming only one conduit which takes the name of *trachea* and climbs vertically to the forward part of the neck.

This *trachea* is a somewhat mobile and stretchable tube, formed of superimposed cartilaginous rings. The diameter of this conduit is about eight to ten twelfths of an inch [eight to ten *lignes*]. It is, in general, proportioned to the volume of the lungs. Above the trachea is placed the *larynx*, with which it is connected. This organ is comprised of several pieces which move on each other, and of which the ensemble can also move with respect to its surroundings, principally in the direction of lowering and raising.

The pieces which compose the larynx, and which are called cartilages, are four in number, namely: the *thyroid*, the *cricoid*, and the two *arytenoids*. The larynx is situated in the forward part of the neck, where it forms a protrusion susceptible to view and touch (the *Adam's apple*). The dimensions of the larynx vary with different individuals in their proportions, which do not always follow those of the height; one observes only that it is more developed and situated lower in men than in women or children. In its entirety, it has somewhat the shape of a cone of which the base is reversed. Its cavity narrows much in the middle, where it presents two horizontal membranes, placed one on the right, the other on the left, and which are called *vocal cords*, or *vocal tendons*.

The opening between these membranes is called the *glottis*, which is why the vocal cords also take the name of *lips of the glottis*. Only that space gives passage to the air which enters and leaves the lungs. Its form is somewhat triangular; scarcely as wide as a few *lignes* at the posterior part, it narrows much at the forward part.

Above the vocal cords are two long hollows which are named the *ventricles of the larynx*, and which are each surmounted by a fold parallel to the vocal cords. These folds leave between them a space called the *superior glottis*.

The movements of the *arytenoid* cartilages can close the posterior extremities of the glottis, and, by narrowing it gradually, make it change from the triangular form which we have just described, until it is only a very narrow fissure which can close itself completely if the lips of the glottis press against each other. These narrowings of the opening, which take place principally during the production of the voice, have the property of making the tones higher and higher. The same thing takes place for the superior glottis, and even for the entire larynx, of which the capacity diminishes noticeably in these same circumstances.

The larynx is terminated by a rather large opening which forms laterally two folds of mucous membrane joined anteriorly to the base of the tongue, and posteriorly to the arytenoid cartilages. These membranes receive the name of *ary-epiglottic membranes* or *folds*. The opening which they leave between them during the act of inspiration is completely closed during the movements of deglutition by a sort of little tongue called the *epiglottis* which is situated behind the tongue.

The voice, while escaping the glottis, goes to reverberate above the larynx, in the *pharynx*, an irregular and very stretchable cavity which extends from the posterior wall, which one sees by lowering the tongue, to the arch which the vertical periphery of the throat forms. The wall at the back of the throat is formed by the muscles called *constrictors*.

The pharynx connects above with the *nasal fossae*. These are two cavities situated above the dividing wall of the mouth and which extend from the pharynx to the nostrils.

It is needless to say that the mouth is bounded at the rear by the pharynx and by the velum, above by the palatal arch, below by the tongue, and on the sides by the cheeks.

The upper part of the mouth is called the *palate*, and the wide and movable partition which terminates the palatal arch posteriorly, the *velum*. The edge of that partition offers a fleshy extension which is called the *uvula*, and which seems to form an archway with two curves.

Departing from the uvula one sees two *frenae* which then descend to form the free edge of the palatal arch. These are the posterior pillars, in front of which are found two others less salient which depart from the same point, the uvula, and which, while descending, separate from the first and leave between them a triangular space where the tonsils are lodged. The opening between the two posterior pillars and the base of the tongue is named the *isthmus of the throat*, or the posterior or *guttural* opening of the mouth.

The pharynx and the mouth are susceptible of receiving the most varied dimensions: the pharynx, because of the movement of the velum, the constrictors, and the base of the tongue; the mouth, because of the movements of the lower jaw.

The description of the other parts of the instrument have been excluded from this sketch. They would be either too far removed from our plan, from the point of view which we have taken [*où nous sommes placés*], or too well known to be detailed here.

EXTRACT FROM THE *MÉMOIRE*

PRESENTED TO THE ACADEMY

CHAPTER I

THE DIFFERENT KINDS OF VOCAL SOUNDS [B]

*The human voice submits to the influence of age, sex, constitu-
tion, and undergoes innumerable modifications. Independent of the out-
standing differences which distinguish the voices of various individuals, there are also an unlimited number of nuances belonging to the
organ of a single individual. In fact, each voice can conform to the
inflections of the most varied passions; it can imitate the cries of
animals and nearly all the sounds which our ears can perceive.*

[C] We have recognized that with the exception of the noises of
the inspiratory voice, all the possible modifications, the cry, the
exclamation, the *high or low* spoken voice, the singing voice throughout its range, *the intensity of the sound;* issue from a small number
of primitive and fundamental principles; by classifying all the similar
facts under a single name, one can establish that the human voice, in
the largest sense, is composed of the different registers: [D]

Chest;

Falsetto-head; [8]

---

[8]The register designated under the name falsetto-head as belonging to a single register, and considered by musicians as formed by two
adjoining registers, of which the lowest takes the name of *falsetto*, or
medium, and the highest takes the name of *head*. In order to be more

Contra-bass;

Of two principal timbres:

The Clear Timbre;

The Sombre Timbre;

[E] And finally, of various degrees of intensity and volume. [F]

THE REGISTERS [G]

By the word register, we understand a series of consecutive and homogenous tones going from low to high, produced by the development of the same mechanical principle, and whose nature differs essentially from another series of tones equally consecutive and homogenous produced by another mechanical principle. All the tones belonging to the same register are consequently of the same nature, whatever may be the modifications of timbre or of force to which one subjects them.

In what follows, we will not include the contra-bass register or the inspiratory voice, two kinds of voice with which we will concern ourselves in separate paragraphs. [H]

*The registers coincide in one part of their compass and follow each other in the other. The tones included in a given compass can belong to two different registers at the same time, and the voice can pass through these tones either in speaking or in singing, without confusing them.

*That takes place for the chest and falsetto which coincide for

---

easily understood, we will make provisory use of that division, reserving until later the demonstration of its inconsistency.

the interval of a twelfth, including from g to d^2.[9]

    *Below and above this compass, each of the two registers extends alone. The total scale of tones through which an individual voice can pass is always composed of the chest and falsetto-head registers, each having a compass which varies, not with the same individual, but from one individual to another.

*The Child's Voice.

    *In childhood, from infancy until the time of puberty, the human voice, identical in girls and boys, presents the complete distinction. between the chest, falsetto, and head registers.

    *The chest register, in principle, rarely extends beyond the fifth, ⟨staff⟩ , but, strengthened by age, it goes beyond it in both directions, and, if it rarely descends below b or $a\#$, ⟨staff⟩ , for compensation, it can reach high tones to c^2 or $c\#^2$. ⟨staff⟩ But also, it is necessary to say, these notes are the result of violent efforts.

---

    [9]The author explained in this footnote the octave notation which he used. Because it is no longer in common usage, we have converted it to the Helmholz notation. In Helmholz's octave notation the octave from middle c to the b above is designated by lower case letters with a superscript *1*; the octave above has the superscript *2*, etc. The octave below middle c is the *small octave*, notated with lower case letters without a superscript; the next lower octave is the *great octave*, notated by capital letters; then the *double octave*, notated by two capital letters.

*This observation is easy to verify with choir boys. Forced to sing at the age of seven to twelve years, in huge buildings and often among masses of formidable voices, they squeal without controlling either their lungs or their throats. It is then that one hears them violently form the tones a^1, b^{b1}, c^2, and $c\#^2$ in the chest, and that one can predict the certain ruin of their voices.

*In this time of life, the vocal organs being small, high-pitched, very supple, and poorly developed, the chest voice, because of this state, shrinks. It is clear, shrill, yelping, moreover, well known under the name of choir boy's voice.

*The falsetto register, much less vital, much weaker than the chest, follows the latter in a compass identical to its own.

*Children generally speak in the falsetto register.

*To these two registers is added the third, or the head voice, which is nothing but the continuation of the falsetto voice. The head voice begins at either $c\#^2$, d^2, or e^{b2}, and upon rising, becomes round, sweet, silvery; it extends to g^2 or to a^2.

*An essential difference which distinguishes this register at every age from the two preceding is that the two previous registers coincide and superimpose, whereas this one touches them end to end, continues them, but does not overlap them.

*The Mutating Voice.

*In proportion with age, which strengthens the organ, the voice
loses its feeble and high-pitched nature. Puberty arrives. Then, for a
few years, there takes place a development which is called mutation.
The children's voices become voices of women and men. During this time
of crisis, it is necessary to let nature, the only dispenser of individual powers, act. In this age of regeneration, the individual could not
be too economical of these powers, nor take too much care of his constitution. If one impoverishes the vocal organ by the practice of singing,
or by any excesses whatsoever, one exhausts the plant before it is fit
to give fruit; one causes decay to succeed childhood.

*It is only after mutation that the serious study of singing
should begin; for girls, from the age of fourteen to sixteen years; for
boys, from seventeen to nineteen years, according to the constitution of
the individual and the influence of the climates. Then, in girls, the
voice has taken some body, some roundness, some range. It has undergone
a still more complete change in the man; it has acquired the masculine
power and it has lowered an octave.*

Women--Chest Voice. ⊤

The chest register is the basic essential of the woman's voice as
of that of the man and child. This register is penetrating, full of
brilliance [éclat]. It follows a range parallel to the falsetto register, but, in its low tones, it can surpass the falsetto by much, since

that register always dies away at $b\flat$ or a, 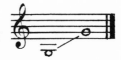 while the

chest tones can descend to $e\flat$. 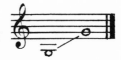 On the top, the range depends

upon the flexibility of the singer. Sometimes it may even reach, as

with children, the extreme limits. Only a few contraltos

reach these limits.

In these exceptional cases, the possible compass of this register

is of a 13th.[10]

Ordinary voices do not go beyond this octave.

Men--Chest Voice.

The chest voice is the fundamental part of the man's voice; it is

loud, round, clear, and ordinarily encompasses two octaves of range. By

joining into a single scale the extremes reached by various individuals,

this register passes through three octaves, bounded by the tones C and

c^2.[11]

It is a curious and interesting fact to record that in men and

women the chest register coincides in the following tones:

---

[10]Madame Malibran, Madame Pisaroni.

[11]Tenors: Haitzinger, Rubini, Duprez; Bass: Porto.

Men always speak in this register; women rarely do so.

Women--Falsetto.

The falsetto belongs particularly to women and children. This register is weak, covered, and rather resembles the low tones of the flute, principally in the lower part. The entire compass is approximately a tenth  .

The more the tones descend below the d^1 , the more they fade; below the a , they cease to sound.

Let us notice that the same compass belongs to the two registers, since, as we have said, one can utter all the tones in the chest voice or in the falsetto voice at will [*indistinctement*]. Women generally speak in the falsetto voice.

Men--Falsetto.

The falsetto, with men, is of the same nature, and placed on the same lines as that of women . But the low tones are difficult to utter and elude the masculine larynx, much better suited to produce the same tones in the chest voice. Sometimes it can begin at: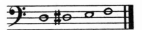

Women--Head Voice.

The head voice, a distinctive and brilliant part of the woman's

voice, marks with its first tone ♪♯♪ , the upper limits of the

two preceding registers. Its range includes:

Men--Head Voice.

Men lose the head voice as a result of mutation; however, some

individuals keep the first major third of it.

Summary.

The chest voice in men extends in its low tones beyond that of

women.

The falsetto voice is common to both men and women.

The head voice of women exceeds that of men.

```
Men's voices          chest
_____
                              |_____| head
                                falsetto

Women's and children's            falsetto          head
    voices                    _____
                                  |_____|
                                    chest
```

_____

[12]Persiani and Demeric can attain these high tones.

*The Contra-Bass Register.

*By this name we designate a series of low and rough [*rauque*] tones, rather similar to the tremolo of the organ or to a strong and sustained swelling. This kind of voice includes the lowest sounds of the basso-profundo, and can extend from the E^b to the fifth below.

*In order to form this range, it is necessary to raise the larynx and enlarge the pharyngeal cavity. The first attempts dry the throat, which brings about coughing movements.

*Comparing this register to the chest register, one sees not only that the tones which compose it differ by their nature from the first, but also that they remain in a much lower region.

*To my knowledge, this register has been used up to now only by some Russian basso-profundos. This register, although it has for the basso-profundos an admirable usage for accompanying other voices, does not seem to me generally applicable to the art of singing, and for two reasons. First, there exists, at least for ordinary voices, a gap between the lowest notes of the chest voice and the tones of the *contra-bass*. This gap could, it is true, disappear in the basso-profundo voices. For them it would be possible not only to join these two parts of the voice, but even to form some tones common to the two registers.

The second inconvenience, and the most troublesome, consists in the deterioration of the other registers which the frequent and pro- longed use of this one unfailingly causes. The Russian basses them- selves justify this observation; after a certain lapse of time there remains for them only the contra-bass voice and a weak section of the chest voice.

*Inspiratory Voice.

It is known that the voice can be formed not only at the time of the exiting of the air enclosed in the chest, but also at the moment the air passes through the larynx to enter the lungs. This inspiratory voice is coarse and unequal, but nevertheless rather extended, especially in the high tones which can even surpass the highest tones of the head register, and that equally for men and women. This kind of voice could not find a place in singing properly so called; reserved exclusively for declamation, it can serve to express certain movements of extreme passion, such as moaning, restrained sighs, etc. But the usage which one can make of this resource must be regulated by the most severe taste.

A General Table

of the possible compass of the human phonator and of each register, except the inspiratory voice.

One sees that we have always placed two or three tones for the limits of each register, because the organs, being elastic, constantly offer this fluctuation.

The human voice, considered as it has just been in all the registers and in every possible range for each of them, offers an interesting development for the physiologist; but the application is here much more restrained than the theory, *and of the different registers which we have recognized, those of the chest, falsetto, and head are the only ones of which the singer should make use.* Yet, they are not all equally natural to use for all singers indiscriminately, and the extreme limits of each are always tiring and scarcely attainable for some artists.

According to the physiologists, the tones are produced when the air contained in the lungs exits, by the result of its action on the lower ligaments of the glottis. The reduction of the ventricles, the reduction of the capacity of the larynx, and the tension of the walls of the vocal tube adapt themselves to the contraction and progressive tension of the vocal ligaments. Until the present, only the production of the chest register has been explained by these principles. The falsetto-head register has been treated only imperfectly; that of the contra-bass has not been studied.

THE TIMBRES [J]

Just as the voice is submitted to the distinctions of the registers, so it is also to the inevitable action of the timbres. We call *timbre* the peculiar and infinitely variable character which each register, each tone, can take, an abstraction made from the intensity.

When the larynx produces a tone, the pharynx takes possession of it as soon as it is emitted and modifies it. [K]

⎣L⎦ Two kinds of conditions control the formation of the timbre: first, the fixed conditions which characterize each individual, those of the form, the consistency, the state of health or illness of the vocal apparatus of each; second, the mobile conditions, such as the direction the sound takes in the vocal tube during its discharge (whether through the nose or through the mouth), the conformation and the degree of capacity of this same tube, the degree of tension of its walls, the action of *the constrictors, that of* the velum, the separation of the jaws and the teeth, the placement of the lips and the dimensions of the opening which they give the mouth, and, finally, the elevation or the depression of the tongue, etc.

In our considerations, we will not concern ourselves with the different timbres which characterize and differentiate the voices of individuals, but only with the diverse timbres which the voice of the same individual presents.

The modifications of timbre, all being produced by two opposite means, can, in the final analysis, be reduced to two principal ones, the *clear timbre* and the *sombre timbre*.

The vocal apparatus cannot produce a sound without dressing it in one or the other timbre, and each timbre imparts its character to the whole range of the voice.

Clear Timbre--Chest Register.

The clear timbre gives to the chest register much lustre and brilliance. In France, this character is expressed by the improper name of "white voice";[13] it would be better to say *white timbre*. *In order to establish our ideas on the clear timbre, on the brilliance and the power that it can allow, I will only cite some examples known to all: the *d* of Mr. Lablache in the finale of *Le Mariage secret*: "Andiam subito a vedere"; the *d*, *e*, *f*, *g*, *a*, of Mr. Levasseur in this phrase from *Robert-le-Diable*: "Eh quoi! tu trembles déjà!"; the *f* of Mr. Rubini in "Il mio tesoro"; the *f* of Garcia at the return of the motive: "Fin che dal vino"; and, finally, the *d* of Mr. Duprez in *Guillaume Tell*. These notes, taken in different parts of the voice, by different singers, are all in chest register and clear timbre.* This timbre carried to exaggeration makes the voice shrill and yelping.

Sombre Timbre--Chest Register.

[M] The sombre timbre, on the contrary, gives in this register some penetration and roundness to the tone. It is with the aid of this timbre that the singer can communicate to his voice all the volume of which it is capable (notice that I speak of volume and not of strength [*force*] or brilliance [*éclat*]). This timbre carried to excess covers the tones, stifles them, makes them muffled and raucous.

The action of the timbres is less salient in the low portion than in the high portion of a register.

The tones included between e^1 and b^1 , when one sings

---

[13]This word means, for the Italians, from whom it was borrowed, the voice of women and children. Through a false idea of timbres, in France, the clear timbre is called *white voice*, as the sombre timbre is called *mixed voice*.

them with full vigor in the chest register and sombre timbre, acquire, in men and women, a dramatic character which has led to an error in the very appreciation of their nature. In place of recognizing in them the influence of the sombre timbre, joined by intensity, in conditions of effect more favorable than anywhere else, people have seen in these tones an exceptional case, and they have designated them by the name *mixed tones*, or *mixed voice, darkened* [*sombrée*]. The *a* string of the violoncello, although weaker, reproduces rather well the same effect.

Clear and Sombre Timbres--Falsetto Register.

In this register, the effect of the timbres, although as definite, is, however, less striking than in the preceding register.

Clear and Sombre Timbres--Head Register.

Although this register is only the continuation of that of the falsetto, it changes name. The cause of this change is the same as we have just indicated for the same tones taken an octave lower in the chest register. The sombre timbre modifies them in a more striking manner, and people have thought they saw a new action where there was only an extension of the same action.

The sombre timbre has in some head voices a most remarkable effect; it makes this register pure and limpid like the sounds of a harmonica.

After having presented a complete description of the voice, we are going to pass on to the study of the mechanical means which serve to produce the timbres.

The Different Positions of the Larynx.

*It is not at all doubtful, after our observations, that the shapes, the diameters, the tension of the walls, the various lengths which the vocal tube assumes are indispensable for the production of the timbres. These conditions are themselves determined: first, by the different positions of the larynx; second, by the corresponding movements of the velum. In fact, the larynx, serving as the base of the vocal tube, must necessarily raise or lower itself to permit this tube to shorten or lengthen itself, and to vary its shape, its diameter, and the tension of its walls.

*We have observed that when the voice passes through each register completely, the larynx behaves very differently in its movements according to whether the series of tones belongs to the clear timbre or the sombre timbre.

*When the voice rises in the chest register from the lowest tone to the highest tone, if the timbre is clear, the larynx occupies in the first moment a position a little lower than that of rest; then, by regular ascending movements, it follows the voice in its rise, carrying itself slightly forward. When the voice reaches the extreme of which it is capable in that register, the larynx moves against the jaw by a very pronounced rocking motion which one can verify by touching it. The tones produced in this last period of the ascension of the larynx are thin and strangled. At the last limits of the compass, the head tips back a little in order to facilitate the elevation of the larynx.

*The same movement is reproduced when the voice passes through the falsetto and head registers in the clear timbre; the larynx takes for its point of departure the same low position as for the lowest note of the falsetto, then it climbs by very slight movements which correspond to the elevation of the tones. As soon as the voice arrives at the head tones, the larynx rises rapidly to the position of deglutition. In this last period the tones are thin and shrill.

*But, if the voice, passing through the chest register, keeps the sombre timbre for all the tones, the larynx remains fixed a little below the position of rest. The lowering becomes especially apparent when the individual seeks, by a last effort, to exaggerate the timbre and to give to his voice all the *volume* of which it is capable. In this last hypothesis, the larynx remains immovably fixed in the lowest position for the entire compass of the register. One is obliged to facilitate this position by leaning the head forward a little. The distinction of the timbres begins to be perceptible only toward d. 𝄢 𝅝 𝄂

*When the larynx produces the falsetto register in the sombre timbre, it again takes the same position as that above, and keeps it unvaryingly, especially if one tries to increase the volume of the voice. As for the head tones, the larynx almost always produces them while rising rapidly. One could not prevent these movements; trying to do so to swell the voice would be a dangerous and often useless effort.

*The slightest modification in the timbre leads necessarily to a change in the position of the larynx. One can be convinced of it by

trying to pass through all the tones alternately from the most open timbre to the most sombre, and one will see the larynx take progressively
higher or lower positions, according to the clearness or the sombreness
of the timbre.

*The movements of the pharynx correspond to the different posi-
tions of the larynx.

*As the pharynx is, of all points of the vocal tube, that which
connects with the most important organs, it is the pharynx also which
can principally fill in its entirety the office of a cavity destined to
modify the sounds emitted by the larynx. The changes in form which the
pharynx can receive being due to the action of the velum and the tongue,
it is especially to the movements of these two organs that the attention
of the singer should be paid.

*First, the velum, placed between the mouth and the nasal fossae,
can cause the dimensions and the form of these openings to change by its
different positions. It can, by presenting itself as a bevel in front
of the column of air, break it and divide it into two currents of air
(of which one will be able to take some nasal resonance, and the other
will flow out through the mouth). These two currents will have a different importance according to the angle of inclination of the palate.
If it rises to the horizontal position, it blocks the posterior opening
of the nasal fossae; then the column of air strikes against the palatal
arch, which presents itself bent at a right angle, and the mouth alone
constitutes the echoing tube. If the velum is completely lowered, the
column of air slides immediately behind it and rises into the nasal

fossae which then offer the only escape for the tone. During these
movements of the velum, the tongue, for its part, always follows the
action of the larynx, to which it is attached. These movements, as well
as those of the larynx, are always executed in the direction opposite
that of the velum; thus, when the velum is bent, the tongue, under the
influence of the larynx which draws it, hollows itself deeply along the
mid line from the posterior part, and the isthmus of the throat presents
the shape of an oval. If the velum lowers, the tongue rises and broadens at the base, and these two organs can approach each other to the
point of touching. The shape which gradually results from this
approaching is rather similar to that of a crescent.

*We have just considered the shapes under which the body of the
instrument can offer itself to the column of air; let us examine now the
points of the tube which the column of air can go to strike, according
as the larynx, by reason of its elevation and of the rocking movements
which it has received, can impart to it a vertical direction or one of
forward inclination.

*When the larynx is lowered, it directs the column of air verti-
cally; when it is raised, it can, by means of the rocking movement which
it has more or less received, direct the column of air either against
the palatal arch, or in front of its velum, or finally, completely forward against the osseous part of the buccal partition.

*That tube through which the tone passes, being able to lengthen
itself and shorten itself, to become more wide or more narrow, being
able to take the form of an ellipse or break itself into a right angle,

being able, finally, to remain in any of the numerous intermediate positions, marvellously fulfils the function of a reflector or megaphone.

    *Now, how is it necessary to use these different movements (of
the larynx and of the throat) in order to impart these different timbres
to the voice?* N

Clear Timbre.

    *When one wishes to produce the clear timbre, beginning with the
first low tone, the pharynx swells more than in the state of rest; but
as soon as the voice leaves that first tone to rise to the upper limits
of the register in clear timbre, all the parts which constitute the
isthmus of the throat tend to come together, following a progressive
course of contraction which corresponds to the gradual rise of the larynx and of the voice. In fact, the velum lowers, and the tongue,
although it depresses along the mid line toward the posterior part,
lifts at the sides and approaches the velum. The form which these movements impart to the resonant tube is that of a flattened arch, of which
the narrow opening is presented immediately above the larynx; this tube
is, moreover, rather short and slightly rounded along its length. The
posterior openings of the nasal fossae are free at this moment because
of the lowering of the velum which is maintained through the entire compass of the register which the clear timbre governs.

    *Meanwhile, the sonorous column, by the inclined direction which
it has received from the larynx, is on its way toward the osseous anterior part of the palate, and the voice, without going to strike in the

nasal fossae, must exit as thrust by the velum, ringing and pure. It is

necessary at this moment to separate the corners of the mouth.

*The vowels [a], [ɛ], [ɔ], *ouvertes à l'italienne*, are modifica-

tions of the clear timbre which bring about this conformation of the

organ.

*The general disposition of the organs, analyzed above, is again

reproduced for the falsetto and head registers; however, the space which

the isthmus of the throat presents is usually less than for the chest

register, a fact which we must attribute in part to the position of the

tongue, which begins to depress along the median line only for the head

tones at the same time as it rises along the sides to the point of

scarcely allowing the uvula to be seen.*

Sombre Timbre.

*The distinction of the timbres, we have said, becomes percepti-

ble only toward d . From that note, the velum rises for the

sombre timbre until the posterior opening of the nasal fossae is com-

pletely closed. The tongue, the base of which is drawn by the lowering

of the larynx, represents an elongated arch, and the sonorous body has

received a long form, bent at a right angle and rather contracted. The

column of air which rises vertically strikes against the palatal arch.

The sound is heard round, full, and covered; it is what is called mixed

voice, or sombre timbre. The vowels [e], [o], *fermées à l'italienne*,

and the vowel [u] are modifications of the sombre timbre which impart these dispositions to the organ.[14]

*Let us observe that, in the two timbres which concern us, the different degrees of force added to the tones do not bring about any perceptible modification in the movements of the organs. The contrary effect is manifested as soon as the singer tries to alter, however little, the nuance of the timbre; the velum lowers for the clear timbre, whereas the sombre timbre produces the elevation of the velum and the enlargement of the pharynx. This enlargement becomes especially percep- tible when the singer gives to his voice all the *volume* which it can allow, although the tones are otherwise very weak; this fact merits being recorded. This exaggeration of volume can take place only in the conditions of the sombre timbre and with violent efforts.

*It is necessary to consider these timbres as the two principal ones, independently of which there exists a great quantity of others, of which, in order to be produced, some borrow from the clear timbre, others from the sombre timbre, whatever these timbres have which is essential in their mechanism. In fact, one observes that the voice can assume some widely varied characters, whether one forms the various vowels and the modifications of which each is susceptible, or one pro- duces the tones under the influence of the emotions. There are not any of these numerous characters which one cannot succeed in reproducing at will after a long practice. [0]

*We are going to study those which, because of their qualities or

---

[14]The vowel [i], not having any character of its own, can receive the two timbres equally.

of their shortcomings, should be known principally to the singer.* P

Guttural Timbre. Q

When the tongue broadens at the base, it presses the epiglottis back onto the column of air, and the voice comes out as though squashed. One can verify this disposition of the tongue by pressing exteriorly on the hyoid bone with the fingers. This last circumstance causes the tone to take a guttural timbre which would not present itself, even under the pressure of the fingers, if the tongue were not swollen [gonflée] at the base.

One sees already that, in order to correct the defectiveness of this timbre, it is necessary to hollow the tongue through the base, and this disposition must be kept, to different degrees, in the emission of all the Italian vowels in order to make them all sonorous. As a consequence, the tongue, which is particularly charged, by its movements, to transform the voice into vowels, will have to be moved, especially by the lateral edges, slightly by the middle, and not at all by the base. Let us add that the separation of the jaws should be approximately uniform for all the vowels. *These conditions fulfilled, all the vowels will be pure and of equal tint.*

Nasal Timbre.

When the vocal apparatus is disposed in the conditions which produce the clear timbre, the voice can receive a nasal character if the column of sonorous air goes directly to take its resonance in the nasal fossae before flowing out through the mouth. [R] It is by pinching the nostrils that one can recognize whether the column of air, as soon as it leaves the larynx, is directed toward the nasal fossae before passing through the mouth, or it proceeds directly toward the latter cavity. *In this latter case the sound will be clear and pure; in the former case the voice will be completely nasal.* [S]

Round Timbre.

When the larynx takes a position a little lower than that for the clear timbre, and the velum rises moderately, the column of air straightens out a little and strikes the middle of the palate. Then the voice is emitted brightly, but more rounded than in the clear timbre. The voice will take some lustre and gain some roundness if the velum is raised still more, so as to leave only a slight communication with the nasal fossae. In this circumstance, the column of air, which is very slightly inclined, strikes in front of the palatal arch.

Harsh [*Rauque*] Timbre.

The voice can become harsh, cavernous, if at the moment the velum is lifted, one increases the separation of the pillars.

The sombre color of the voice will always be increased if one presents an obstacle to the sound waves. Thus, the lifting of the tongue at the tip or the bringing together of the lips is sufficient to produce this effect.

The swelling of the tonsils can also muffle the voice by acting

as an obstacle. Young persons often present an example of this fact.
It is accompanied in them by difficulty in forming and extending the
head voice. Moreover, this difficulty is common to all women's voices
in the state of fatigue.

One can also muffle the voice by expending the air inordinately.
Suffocated sounds and deep sighs are examples of it. The excessive air
rubs the walls of the instrument and gives rise to a noise which con-
tributes to the dulling of the tones.

One understands that there will be as many shades in these timbres as there are varieties in the combination of the mechanical conditions which we have just described.

Intensity and Volume. ⊤

*Although intensity and volume are often found joined, it is
necessary not to confuse them. The increase of force does not lead to
the augmentation of volume; a tone can be weak and big at the same
time.*

The intensity of the voice depends first upon the presence of a
resonant body. It is known, in fact, that the vibrations of a string or
the mouthpiece of a wind instrument, isolated, always produce a thin
sound, and that in order to enlarge it, it is necessary to join the
mouthpiece or the string to an instrumental body which vibrates, with
the body of air which it contains, in unison with the vibrator. Likewise, the larynx, separated from the pharynx, would produce only thin
and shrill tones. The capacity of the vocal cords to vibrate, the

dimensions of the larynx, the thorax, the lungs, the pharyngeal, buccal, and nasal cavities, the disposition of these same cavities to resonate, constitute the absolute power of the voice of an individual.

The physicists attribute intensity to the stronger or weaker compressions that the air has received from the resonant body. So, the more force with which the air will be pushed from the chest, the wider the vibrations of the vocal cords will be.

The volume of the tone always requires, whatever the degree of intensity may be, a large pharyngeal capacity and the lowered position of the larynx; that-is-to-say, the conditions of the sombre timbre.

Thus, then, intensity and volume differ in that the first depends upon the greater or lesser emission of the air and the amplitude of the vibrations which it can impart to the vocal cords; the second, upon the capacity of the resonant body.

*In order to summarize in a few words these ideas on the voice and its modifications, we will say that the instrument in which the human voice is produced is formed of three parts, each of which has its own mode of action, namely:

A bellows or air duct (lungs and trachea);

A vibrator (larynx);

And a reflector or modifier of the tone (pharyngeal, nasal, and buccal cavities).

The singer, to dominate the material difficulties of his art, must have a thorough knowledge of the mechanism of all these parts to the point of isolating or combining their actions, according to need.

THE SCHOOL OF GARCIA

First Part

THE TRAINING OF THE PHONATOR

CHAPTER I

GENERAL OBSERVATIONS

1. APTITUDES OF THE STUDENT [A]

*In the investigation which we are going to outline of the quali-
ties most necessary to the student, we have in view the singer who
intends to take up opera. Not only should he have the intellectual
advantages which will permit him to satisfy all the demands of a severe
criticism, but also, his constitution should enable him to withstand the
wear and tear which await him in the practice of his art.*

The most favorable intellectual conditions are a true passion for
music, the capacity to grasp clearly and to engrave into his memory the
melodies and harmonic combinations, *an exuberant spirit, joined with a
quick and observing mind.* With respect to the physical conditions, we
place in the first rank the voice, which should be fresh, attractive
[sympathique], extensive, and strong; in the second rank the vigor of
the constitution, usually matched to the qualities of the organ which we
have just indicated. [B]

*Thus should every individual be organized who wishes to rise to
the rank of distinguished artist,* but let one make no mistake about it,
the combination of all these natural gifts, however rare they may be,

would not suffice by themselves to constitute true talent. The most favorable aptitudes need to be cultivated and directed in their application by a sustained and orderly labor. The singer who ignores the sources of the effects and the secrets of the art is only an incomplete talent, a slave of routine.

It does not suffice to grasp some hasty notions about music; artists are not improvised; they are formed over a long time; it is necessary that their talent be developed early by a general education and by special studies. *We will say only a word more about a refined schooling; the artist whose mind is not cultivated would have difficulty grasping the whole of a role, to understand the scope of it, and to discover in it the characteristic traits which impart a true and original mark to a character of the drama.*

The special training of the singer is composed of the study of solfeggio, of that of an instrument, and, finally, of the study of singing and of harmony. This last science is an indispensable resource for the singer. It is with its help that the singer can adapt roles to his own voice, ornament them, bring out the beauties in them, all the while respecting the character which is proper to them and adding his own genius to that of the composer. Only the knowledge of harmony can enable him to vary his songs without preparation, whether to renew the effect of them, or to avoid artistically the difficulty of a passage when a sudden indisposition deprives him of part of the range of his voice.

This last test, which presents itself rather frequently in a theatrical career, exposes the learning of a singer and is unfavorable only to ignorance. *In fact, the singer unprepared in harmony [*le simple orecchiante*], deprived of a part of his means in an occasion so exacting, can render only incompletely the thought of the composer or disfigure it while wishing to change it, and in either case he exposes himself to the mockery of his audience.

*Often one needs an experienced judgement to recognize in the voice of the student the germ of the true qualities which it possesses. Generally, these qualities are only in the rudimentary state, or well-veiled by numerous faults from which it is necessary to free them.

The essential point is to first establish the existence of them; one then manages to complete the development of them by patient and orderly studies.

Voices in their natural states are nearly always unpolished [*rude*], unequal, unsteady, even tremulous, and, finally, heavy and of short range; only study, but a well-informed and persistent study, can make firm the intonation, purify the timbres, perfect the intensity and the elasticity of the tone. Through study, one can smoothe the harshnesses, the disparities of the registers, and by uniting them to each other, one can extend the scope of the voice. Study will make us acquire agility, a quality generally too much neglected, *especially in Italy.* It is necessary to submit to rigorous exercise not only the stubborn organs, but also those which, drawn along by a dangerous facility, cannot control their movements. That apparent flexibility is connected to lack of clarity, steadiness [*tenue*], balance, and breadth; that-is-to-say, to the absence of all the elements of accent and style.

*It is necessary to guard against criticizing students too severely, even those who are appearing in the troublesome circumstances of a debut. The only faults which should make one despair of their success are:

A limited intelligence;

An uncertain [*fausse*] voice and ear;[15]

A voice partially or entirely hoarse [*rauque*] or tremulous.

*Whether this last tendency is normal or whether it is revealed after a short exercise, the person who presents it has little hope for success.

*The pupil whose voice remains high-pitched, broken, and weak, even after mutation is completed, should renounce the singing profession. We will say the same for any person whose throat is constantly inflamed. One rather often recognizes there a considerable swelling of the tonsils, and the voice always feels the effects of that illness, although the larynx and lungs remain healthy; for it is wrong to think, as one generally does, that a strong chest always means a firm and full voice; the organs of phonation should be equally vigorous.

*It is also necessary to renounce success for persons with weak and sickly constitutions; a delicate health never permits the artist to

---

15This imperfection proves neither the inability to form correct tones nor a defective conformation of the ear which would not at all permit the distinct perception of tones; it denotes only an insufficient musical intelligence. It is evident that one should not conceive an unfavorable prejudice against a student who sings out of tune in the study of the first exercises. One should declare that fault hopeless only after several months of attempts to correct it.

communciate energy, the prime characteristic of emotion, to the tone.*

2. EXCESSES

Of all the instruments, the human voice is the most delicate and the most fragile. Ⓒ *The organs which serve to produce it, being submitted to the double influence both of the general causes of health or of illness, and of all the various emotions which stir us, are exposed to a thousand different attacks [*atteintes*].* Singers, so strongly interested in the preservation of their instruments, will understand the necessity of the detailed cares which should prevent the alteration or the total loss of them.

First, they should avoid excesses of all kinds: **of diet, habits, or conduct.** There is none which does not immediately exercise a deadly action on the organs of the voice. In order to limit ourselves here to the abuse which the singer can do to his means by singing itself, we will point out as dangerous: (1) the too frequent use of the high tones in the chest and head registers; (2) the excessive force which one would impart to the voice; (3) the exaggeration of the timbres, principally in songs sung in full voice and in the high tones. Of the two timbres, the one of which the exaggeration brings about the worst effect is the sombre timbre, because of the efforts which it requires of the muscles of the pharynx; (4) finally, laughing with the throat spread [*deployée*], the word sustained for a long time with ardor, screams, loud cries [*vociférations*]. All these excesses fatigue the organ, make it hoarse momentarily, and, if often repeated, will not fail

6

to destroy it.[16] This result would be infallible if the same impru-
dences were committed in the open air, particularly under the influence
of the cold and humid air of evening.

[D] Freshness, spontaneity, **and firmness** are the most valuable qualities of the voice, but they are also the most fragile. The
voice which loses them never regains them; the timbre of it remains
hopelessly cracked. A voice which has been reduced to that point of
exhaustion is called *worn out*, or *broken* [*cassée*]. **One such exhaustion of forces is manifested sometimes from the beginning of the period
of study, and when it is not due to illness, one can attribute it to the
bad direction given to the studies of the student. The error would be
equally deplorable whether the teacher misunderstood the nature of the
organ or whether one aspired, by a stubborn labor, to change the voice
from low to high. This last attempt would result in the inevitable
destruction of the voice. Study should tend to develop the natural
gifts of the organ, not to change them or extend them inordinately.**

*A simple lack of moderation in poorly directed work is often
sufficient to expose one to consequences no less grave.*

3. PRECAUTIONS

*Some distinguished singers are in the habit of practicing on a
piano whose pitch is lower than that which instrument makers usually
employ and which custom has introduced into the orchestras. A passage

---

*[16]Lawyers, preachers, orators, military commanders, and children
at play offer us frequent proof of these last observations.*

repeated often would become too fatiguing without this precaution; students who prefer not to adopt this procedure will do well to have recourse to transposition.

*The prolonged study of any instrument whatever, as well as too violent body exercise, exhausts the voice.

*The singer will avoid sudden transitions of temperature, and especially of humidity, which could cause him to catch colds and hoarseness.

*The practice of singing at times too close to meals injures the digestion and impairs the health.

*To sing in a dull apartment, or opposite an obstacle, such as a vertical piano, a tapestry, a wall, etc., is to expose oneself, to no purpose, to a great fatigue of the lungs and the throat.

*Irritating foods, oils contained in certain dried fruits, exciting drinks, are injurious to the organ. The food of the singer should be wholesome and simple. It is evident that one should suspend work the moment one experiences the slightest pain in the throat.

Since it is important that the singer maintain all the freedom of movement of the face which will permit him to express all the various nuances of emotion, no contortion, no annoying habit contracted in his studies should hinder this ability; we urge him therefore to place himself before a mirror in order to avoid the movements of the body, the eyebrows, the eyelids, the forehead, the head, the mouth, and, in general, every gesture and every grimace which would sully his talent.

4. GENERAL OBSERVATIONS ON THE MANNER OF STUDY [E]

*Since the student should apply himself, before all, to acquiring a faultless accuracy of intonation--that-is-to-say, to attain the exact relationship between the tones which form any interval whatever--it is important that the piano by which he practices leave nothing to be desired in the perfection of its tuning; we insist upon this necessity, generally too little stressed. The student should find a secure guide in the instrument which accompanies him and should not exercise his voice without using [consulter] it.[17]

*An applied instrumentalist studies his instrument four, six, or eight hours each day, and if sure and methodical principles guide his labor, he will not delay in seeing it crowned with prompt success. If the singer followed such a system, his instrument, incomparably more fragile, would succumb under such an effort and would be promptly exhausted. The musician can exchange his used instrument, but the singer who loses his voice loses it forever.

*It is necessary, therefore, to practice moderately and to precede the physical work with mental work, in order to avoid the gropings which, instead of being sources of progress, serve only to fatigue the

---

[17]"A famous singer whom I saw in Rome (says Grétry, Essais sur la Musique, I, 268), Gizziello, would send his tuner into the house where he wanted to show his talents, not only from fear that the harpsichord might be too high, but also for the perfection of the intonation [accord]." Gioacchino Conti, who took for himself the surname Gizziello, as a mark of gratitude for the help which he had received from his master, Domenico Gizzi, was one of the greatest singers of the eighteenth century, and the rival of Farinelli.

organ, even the most robust.*

In the first days, the students should not devote themselves to practicing more than five consecutive minutes at a time; however, the short periods can be repeated four or five times each day, separated by long intervals. Then the time devoted to the work can be increased by five minutes at a time, to be extended to a half hour, a limit which should never be surpassed. At the end of five or six months, one will be able to do four of the half-hour practices per day, but one will take care never to go beyond that; it is still well understood that these half hours will be separated by long rests.

One will begin the daily study with the emission of the voice. *We will return to that point in the article which treats of it in a special manner.*

We will not concern ourselves at first with the *messa di voce*, which we believe needs to be treated only in one of the advanced chapters of this first part. *To spin out the tones [*messa di voce*] is to refine [*polir*] them, to give them their final polish [*vernis*]. In order to succeed in it, it is necessary to master the action of the lungs and that of the pharynx.* The study of the *messa di voce*, if one indulged in it at the beginning, would succeed only in fatiguing the student without teaching him anything. The ability to spin out tones should in a way be the result of all the other studies; to be able to spin out tones well is to be a singer. F

*The exercises should regularly be studied in full voice, for it is more difficult to develop the intensity of the tones than to restrain

it. Is it necessary to warn that in imparting some fullness to the voice one should neither overly enlarge [*grossir*] it, not force it, nor make it harsh and shrill?

*The high tones of the head register in women and those of the chest register in men should ordinarily be mellow and rounded.

*All voices cannot attain the same degree of agility. One will be content to give the instrument of the student its final development of relative celerity. The more clear, white, thin, and supple the voices are, the more agile they can become, and *vice versa.**

Sopranos should attain the speed of ♩ = 132 on the Maelzel metronome.

We have classified the exercises in the order which seemed to us most logical. That order can be reversed by the teacher, who will change the arrangements of the exercises or leave out some according to the ability and the needs of the student.

As soon as the chest voice is developed and the student can pass from that register to that of the falsetto while bringing out the passage very distinctly, it will be necessary to begin the exercises.

Although the exercises of this method are written in a single key, usually the key of *C*, it will be necessary to transpose them successively into the various keys in order to exercise the entire compass of the voice equally, but never surpassing the easy limits. It is clear that each voice should be exercised in keys corresponding to its range.

When an exercise is complicated for a student, he should simplify it by writing it out in all the keys in which his voice can perform it.

This work avoids long gropings and familiarizes him quickly with the forms of the passages.

*The teacher will do well to vary the harmony of the accompaniments in order to strengthen the intonation from the beginning.

While having a student study, it is not necessary either to play his part on the piano or to smother his voice with the strength of the accompaniment. It will be well to stop the accompaniment from time to time; this procedure makes the defects in the performance more noticeable and easier to point out.

All the exercises should be performed in regular meter; but when the development of them is continuous, the student, **instead of breathing in a jerky and noisy manner in the middle of a passage,** *should stop after the first note of the measure* and make use of the rest to inhale; then he will resume the passage on the tone at which he has just stopped. Thus the examples:

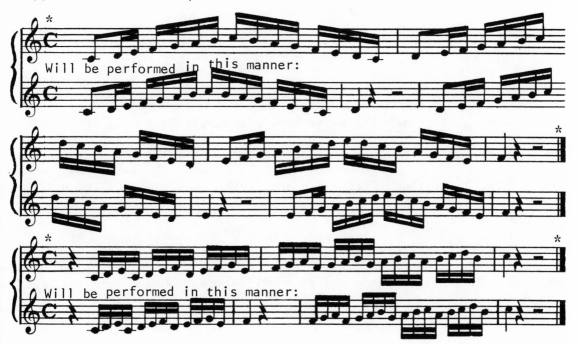

Will be performed in this manner:

The exercises will at first be sung slowly and interrupted with frequent breaths; then the increasing facility of the student will permit him to accelerate the performance, to inhale less frequently, **and, finally, to recite the passages at full speed and with a single breath.** In any case, he will not extend the duration of the breath beyond its natural limit.

*I require that he apply himself to this procedure in order to familiarize himself with the long breath, which is most important. The omission of this study would make the breath hurried [*précipité*], noisy, short, and jerky.* He should not allow his surplus air to escape on the note on which he stops. *The action of the chest should always be elastic and gentle [*léger*].*

*In all the exercises, one should require the following qualities:

*One will attack the tones purely and by a *coup de glotte* which is proportional to the intensity of the tone.

The intonation will be perfect, invariable, lasting the entire duration of the tone.

One will strictly maintain all the tones **in the same timbre, as well as** in an equal force and in equal values.

*The vowel adopted will be maintained purely and without

alteration.

*The timbre will depend upon the vowel; it is up to the teacher to choose the one which suits the student. The tone needing to be full and sonorous, open and lightly rounded vowels should generally be adopted by preference.

*For the tones of the third register one will choose the sombre timbre.

*The agility will be both connected [*liée*] and distinct; that is the proper nature of vocalization; the other modes are only the means of coloration.*

When the voice can be sustained purely on the vowel [a], it will be time to exercise on the other vowels: [e], [ɛ], [o], [ɔ] (see Part Two). The vowels [i] and [u] will be studied also, but only as much as will be necessary to accustom the voice to them. ☐G

*In general, tenors and women will connect the vocalization; basses and sombre, covered voices will be careful to mark it.

*In order to maintain a perfect regularity in the time and in the values, one will make use of the Maelzel metronome.[18] One will use it immediately after having triumphed over the first difficulties. That instrument serves at the same time to make the performance more rapid and more regular. One will begin slowly and will accelerate the

---

18The divisions of that instrument are based on the duration of one minute. Each numeral indicates the number of oscillations which the pendulum will execute during that lapse of time; for example, when the weight is fastened on number 60, each oscillation of the pendulum will equal one second.

14

movement only when the passage is pure and correct.

      *Whatever passage one performs, one will take care not to neglect or avoid the bold and pronounced passage from the chest register to the falsetto register, and *vice versa*. It is by approaching that difficulty frankly each time it is presented that one will succeed in making it familiar and in conquering it with ease. I advise here to choose by preference the clear timbre, avoiding, however, making it guttural, a danger to which one is immediately exposed.* ⊞

CHAPTER II

THE CLASSIFICATION OF CULTIVATED VOICES [A]

1. WOMEN'S VOICES

The woman's voice, more beautiful and more supple than that of the man, is the supreme interpreter of melody. The range, the strength, and the character of the woman's voice vary according to the conformation of the individual **organs.** They have been classified, according to that conformation, into four groups:

The *contraltos*, who occupy the lowest step of the vocal range;

The *mezzo-sopranos*, who occupy the middle of it, about a third above the *contraltos*;

The *sopranos*, placed about a third above the *mezzo-sopranos*;

And the *extra-high sopranos* [*soprani sopri-acuti*], who occupy the summit of the scale, a third above the *sopranos*; they are very rare.

All the normally formed women's voices possess all three of the registers.

Contralto Voice.

Contralto voices are usually masculine and energetic in the chest register. The power, roundness, **penetrating sound, and expressiveness** of this register are its distinctive qualities. **This register is not as powerful or as low in the *mezzo-sopranos* as in the *contraltos*,

and still less so in the *sopranos*.** However, it is the essential basis
of the woman's voice, as of that of the man and child. *This register,
neglected, or perhaps misunderstood, by some teachers, especially in
France, remains ignored with many students. Thus, one is deprived of
the most valuable resource of the voice.* **Every human voice possesses
it, and it would be a gross error to deny this physiological fact. This
register can, if one takes into consideration the lowest notes of the
voice,** extend from: [19]

   **However, whatever the lower note at which one begins this reg-
ister, one must always stop it at without ever surpassing
that point.** *The tones indicated in quarter notes in the above example are produced with difficulty and are dangerous to try; few persons
have an organ which is flexible enough to form them and enough judgement
to use them only where appropriate. It would be imprudent to aspire to
obtain them contrary to nature.* **Attempts to obtain them could cause
the loss of the voice.**

   [B] The falsetto extends from , but the portion of
that range from is weak and cannot be sustained at the
same degree of force as the corresponding range in the chest register.

_____

   19Madame Pisaroni.

*That is why we substitute the chest register for the falsetto, as one will see later.

*The following tones  have intensity and character if one practices them right away before the forced study of the same tones in the chest register has muffled them in this register.

The head register extends from [music] to [music] . This last register is very fatiguing for the contraltos; one should approach these tones only by touching them lightly in passages. All songs which hold them in a sustained manner would become unperformable.

Mezzo-Soprano Voice.

*The three registers extend as the following example indicates:

Chest   Falsetto   Head

[music] Sometimes they arise and descend more; for example: [music] but the tones of the lower third, as well as the high tones, are somewhat exceptional.[20]

*This kind of voice offers great resources for musical coloring, for if it does not have the power of the contralto or as much spontaneity in the high range as the soprano, it has more fullness than the latter in the middle and low and more facility in the high than the first. Mezzo-soprano voices are, or can become, equal and full throughout their

----

[20]Madame Malibran.

range by the use of the three registers.*

Soprano Voice.

The soprano voices shine primarily by the facility and the spontaneity of the head register. *These voices are brilliant, nimble,
ringing;* their power is in the high tones; they are weak in the low
ones. Their range is as follows:

*The tones in this lowest fifth are dull and

extremely weak; it is absolutely necessary, therefore, to substitute for
them the corresponding tones in the chest register, which, although they
do not have much power, do not lack bite [*mordant*]. The tones of the
upper falsetto are weak but pure.* One has already seen that all the
women's voices have a similar part, the falsetto register, identical in
range, different in intensity and beauty.

2. MEN'S VOICES

Having regard for the range, the character, *and the power* of
the men's voices, they have been classified in the following order:

---

*21 The tones d^3, e^3, and f^3 are rare. I have heard Mademoiselle
Sontag and Madame Persiani produce the d^3 and the e^{b3}, but I have heard
the f^3 only in the voice of Madame Demeric at the time of her debut in
1816. The voice of that artist was, as one says, an instrument of
unequalled beauty and purity.*

The *basso-profundos*, who occupy the bottom of the **vocal** scale;

The *baritones*, who are placed a third above the *bassos*;

The *tenors*, who begin a third above the *baritones*;

The *counter-tenors* [*haute-contre*, *contraltino*], who occupy the summit of the scale, a third above the *tenors*.

Basso-Profundo Voice.

The bassos can be satisfied with the chest register.

The sonorous and voluminous voice of the basso extends:[22]

Basso-profundos have difficulty in attacking the falsetto tones; *the head tones are completely lacking to them.* Fashion, which controls everything, by a deplorable caprice has almost excluded them from the theaters today. They are being replaced by baritones.

Baritone Voice.

This voice, less voluminous than the preceding, is full and sono-

rous. It extends:

All the baritones, as well as the tenors and the counter-tenors,

---

[22]Mr. Porto at the Italian Theater, and Mr. Levasseur at the Opera.

have the ability to form the tones of the falsetto. It has for them the
same range as it does for women. However, few baritones will use it
successfully.

Tenor Voice.

These voices, less voluminous than those preceding, *have more
roundness and* are more sonorous, more fluent [*facile*] in the high

part. Their range is rarely of two octaves: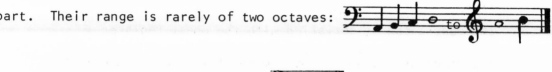

*The tones in this interval ![notation] are weak, while the cor-
responding tones of the mezzo-soprano and contralto voices are ringing
and full.*

The falsetto united with the chest register is, for the tenors
more than for the baritones, a successful and natural resource. The
much too elevated tessitura of the music composed today for tenors does
not permit them to do without the falsetto register. But the use of
that resource, however, should be determined by the ability of the organ
to blend together the metals [1872: timbres] of the two registers;
otherwise, however well-conceived the transition between the registers
may be, the disparity of the sounds would shock the ear and destroy the
unity of the effect; one would think one was hearing two different individuals singing alternately in the same phrase.

The head voice, offering a still more striking contrast with the
chest voice, will also be used with more reservation.

Counter-Tenor Voice.

The highest voice of the man. This clear and nimble voice, whose range is the same as that of the contralto voice, and is composed of the same cords, extends from  .[23]

In this voice, the chest register blends very well with the falsetto register, but, although more thin and more effeminate than all the other masculine voices, it blends poorly [*forme une disparate*] with the head register, which is exclusively reserved for the woman.

TABLE OF THE CLASSIFICATION OF **CULTIVATED** VOICES

23Mr. Rubini, Mr. Haitzinger.

The classical range allowed in the Italian schools for all the

voices was   . (a   The rest of the possible range, above and

below, was left to the singer.

One sees in the table above two or three tones as the limit of

each register because the human voice always offers that margin of

fluctuation.

---

a) The interval of the twelfth without a clef sign briefly
confused the translator; then he looked again at Garcia's chart and
realized that for each voice classification one merely adds the clef
sign corresponding to that voice.

CHAPTER III-A

THE FORMATION OF TONES (b

By means of what mechanism is the voice formed? *The voice is formed only by the periodic compressions and expansions* [dilatations] *which the air experiences when, at its exit from the glottis, that organ, by a regular and alternating action, stops it and allows it to pass.*

As a matter of fact, the two little lips which, in the larynx, form between them a passage for the breath (the glottis), adhere to each other and cause a certain accumulation of air. That air, by virtue of the elasticity which it acquires due to the pressure exerted upon it, separates the lips of the glottis, and, expanding, exits with a burst. But, at the same instant, relieved of the pressure from below and pulled by their own elasticity, the lips meet again to give rise to a new explosion. From this series of successive and regular contractions and expansions or explosions is born the emission of the voice. One can form a very correct idea of it by considering in what manner the lips of the mouth act when they make tones against the mouthpiece of a horn.

Upon the rapidity of the alternations which the glottis presents to the air depends that of the explosions, and upon that, the pitch of

---

b) This chapter appears to have been added to Garcia's method after his investigations with the laryngoscope in 1854 and 1855. It seemed too important to Garcia's presentation to relegate it to an extended note in the collation appendix; therefore, we chose to present it as an interpolated chapter near the position which it occupied in the 1872 edition.

the tone. These alternations are as much more rapid as the dimensions of the vibrating orfice are more short.[24] Now here is the procedure by which the glottis shortens its dimensions: as soon as it produces a tone, it passes from the triangular form, that of rest, to the linear form, that of action. Its sides, fixed solidly and put into contact by their extremities, leave an elliptical space only toward the middle when the air separates them. Of these extremities, only the posterior ones, constituted of cartilages, have the privilege of moving, and of opening the glottis by withdrawing from each other, or else to close it by touching each other. The anterior extremities are always fixed. If one produces the lowest tone of the voice, the sides of the glottis are involved [*comprennent*] throughout their length, that-is-to-say, the cartilage and the tendon which is a continuation of it (see page 205); but, as soon as the voice begins to rise, the contact of the cartilages, limited at first to their posterior extremity, progresses [*gagne*] by extending from the rear to the front until the two cartilages are in contact throughout their length. This movement has decreased the length of the glottis accordingly until it corresponds to the length of the tendons alone. Those, obeying themselves, in their turn, the progressive

---

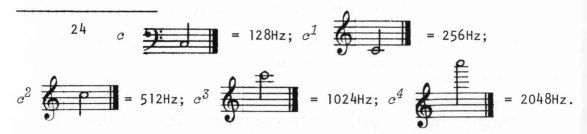

24 c = 128Hz; c^1 = 256Hz; c^2 = 512Hz; c^3 = 1024Hz; c^4 = 2048Hz.

Each octave requires a number of vibrations double that of the octave below.

movement, further reduce the dimensions of the vibrating part.

1. THE FORMATION OF THE REGISTERS

We shall limit ourselves here to presenting to the student some observations with an immediate application.[25] The chest voice, which possesses much more brilliance than the falsetto, also requires a more vigorous *pinching* of the glottis. This pinching, which one obtains easily with the vowel [i], is the procedure which one must indicate to women in order to make them find the chest voice. The falsetto voice, ordinarily the more veiled of the two, also causes a larger expenditure of air. Both registers, for the low tones, place the entire length of the glottis into vibration; then, as we have just said, the gradual rise of the tones gives rise to a more and more extensive contact of the cartilages. When the contact is complete, only the tendons continue to vibrate, and then there appears, in tenors, a very distinctive range comprised between the e^1 and the c^2 , called by some musicians the mixed voice or half chest [*mezzo petto*], and, in women, the head register, which is placed an octave above. Both are produced exclusively by the vocal tendons.

At the moment when the tendons are about to circumscribe the glottis by themselves, but when the summits of the cartilages are still

---

[25]For the full details, see the *Observations* made on the human voice, which I presented on March 22, 1855, to the Royal Society of London. *Proceedings of the Royal Society*, VII, 13. I [Garcia] have published a French translation of that tract.

involved [*engagés*] in the vibrations, these summits do not always press against each other as firmly as the vibrations require, and, in the tones between b^1 and $d\#^2$ in women's voices, or between b and $d\#^1$ in men's voices, the instability of the glottis causes the voice to be weak and uncomfortable. But, as soon as the cartilages are no longer vibrating, which happens for women at e^2 , and for men at e^1 , the tones become pure and perfectly placed. The very pronounced *pinching* of the glottis will be the remedy for the weakness which we have just pointed out.[26]

[26]When sopranos want to emit the tones b^2 or c^3, it sometimes happens that the voice jumps by itself to the d^3 or e^3, and these high-pitched tones, supple [*délié*] and pure in character, cost them less effort than the lower tone which they were trying to reach. Here is the mechanism from which these tones result:

The lips of the glottis are taut and accurately, but gently touching each other; the space between the superior vocal tendons is constricted [*resserré*]. In this position of the organs it sometimes requires only the least pressure of the air for it to pass through the glottis via an extremely tiny fissure, and that narrow opening produces very rapid vibrations with great facilty. One imagines that the pressure of the air should be as light as possible if one wishes to keep the dimensions of the glottis small.

The procedure which we have just described, used with success by certain female voices, can be used equally by certain male voices. It serves in that case to lighten relatively high tones of basses which are often too thick; it also offers tenors a means of increasing the range of the chest register and of singing its high notes in *mezza voce*.

2. NUANCES OF *BRILLIANCE* AND *DULLNESS* OF THE VOICE

It is not necessary that the glottis be hermetically closed after each time it is partially opened; it is enough that it oppose the air with a contraction capable of developing its elasticity. Only the noise of the air escaping through the orifice, which is constantly partly open, will be heard and will give the voice a veiled and sometimes dull quality, a phenomenon which one frequently notices in the falsetto register. Consequently, it is necessary to conclude that the brilliance of the voice results from the firm closure of the glottis after each pulsation. This procedure also has the advantage of bringing about a great economy of the air. We urge students to immerse [*se pénétrer*] themselves well in these observations; they are of the utmost importance.

3. THE INTENSITY AND VOLUME OF THE TONES

The intensity of the tone depends upon the quantity of air which makes each lively explosion [*explosion vive*]. I say lively explosion as an express condition; that-is-to-say, that the glottis should close hermetically after each vibration; for, as we have just seen, if the air found a constant outlet, then the largest excursions of the glottis and the strongest expenditure of air would produce precisely the weakest tones. It is necessary to pinch the glottis in proportion to the amount of pressure one gives the air.

The volume depends upon the amount of separation which the superior tendons form above the glottis.

4. THE FORMATION OF THE TIMBRES

Various simultaneous causes can modify the timbres of the voice:
(1) according as the glottis narrows or partially opens, it produces
ringing or lustreless tones; (2) the superior tendons, which surround
the glottis, if they open, give volume to the tone, and if they narrow,
they disturb the movements of the glottis and produce a sort of stifled
effect in the voice; (3) the pharynx, in its turn, imparts to the tones
which pass through it the variable characteristics of the timbres and
the vowels.

As soon as the tone is formed, it immediately comes under the
influence of the vocal tube through which it passes.

This tube, being able to elongate or to shorten itself, to
broaden or to narrow itself, to take the form of a slight curve or to
break into a right angle, and finally, to maintain any of the numerous
intermediary forms, fulfils wonderfully the functions of a reflector or
a megaphone.

One conceives therefore that there will be as many nuances in the
timbres as there are varieties in the combinations of those mechanical
conditions.

In order to understand well the movements of the pharynx, it is
necessary to imagine a deep and extensible tube which begins at the larynx, curves at the palatal arch, and ends at the opening of the mouth.
This tube can shorten, and then it describes only a slight curve; or it
can lengthen, and then it breaks into a right angle. In the first case,

the larynx rises toward the velum, and the velum lowers toward the larynx; in the second case, that-is-to-say, when the tube elongates, the
larynx lowers and the velum rises.

The short and slightly curved form produces the clear timbre; the
elongated and strongly curved form produces the sombre timbre.

There is an intimate relationship between the various vowels and
the various conformations of the pharynx; we will do a special article
on that when we treat the fourth mechanism.

The body of observations which the study of the timbres has furnished to us can be summed up in a single principle formulated thus:
*Each modification introduced into the mode of producing the vibrations
engenders a different timbre, and each modification which the tube of
transmission undergoes modifies the original timbre.*

THE TIMBRES boxed(A)

*The timbres become very distinct only on and above d [musical notation] .
Their divergence increases as the pitch ascends.*

1. THE CLEAR TIMBRE

The clear timbre is the only one which makes the voice supple
[*déliée*] and penetrating. Although it can impart its character to the
entire range of the voice, it is especially in this tenth of the chest
register [musical notation] that it exerts the most action. Basses
should abandon it at the d^1 [musical notation] exclusively.[27] boxed(B)

*Carried to exaggeration, this timbre makes the voice shrill
[*aigre*], squalling [*criarde*], yelping [*glapissante*].

*One obtains the high tones of the chest register more easily in
the clear timbre than in the sombre timbre. The former allows the
throat all possible flexibility and freedom.*

---

*[27]It makes the voices of some singers brassy, metallic, power-
ful: for example, that of Mr. Levasseur in this phrase: *"Eh quoi! tu
trembles déjà?"* Also Mr. Lablache, in these words from the finale of
The Secret Marriage: *"Andiam subito a vedere,"* produced a gigantic d^1

[musical notation] . Mr. Rubini, in *"Il mio tesoro intanto,"* and Garcia, in his
reentry of the motive, *"Fin ch'an dal vino,"* have given an f^1 [musical notation]
which will not be easily erased from the memories of the
dilettanti.*

2. THE SOMBRE TIMBRE

*The sombre timbre makes the chest voice round, full, and sweet. Each register allows in this timbre all the volume which the individual can impart to the organ. The tones $f\#^1$ through b^1 especially acquire in both sexes an admirable penetration [*mordant*]. It is in this timbre that one must use them in passages of great energy, when the same tones in falsetto would be weak and colorless. Few tenors or contraltos can attempt the tones above a^1 with impunity.

*The distinction between the registers and the timbres never having been well-established or well-analyzed, the masculine and dark vigor which the high tones of the chest register acquire in the timbre which concerns us has been wrongly appraised. It has given rise to a thousand discussions and to some bizarre nomenclatures which have confused teachers and students.

*The range of the fourth indicated above has been named *mixed voice*: that-is-to-say, chest and falsetto registers at the same time; others have named it the *medium voice*, borrowing that name from its position in the range. It ought to have been named *chest voice in sombre timbre*, and one would have understood that it was imprudent to force oneself to obtain it at any price.

*The clear and sombre timbres are suitable to the falsetto when they are pure and free [*franc*]; the first gives it brilliance [*éclat*], the second, body and resonance. The action of the sombre timbre on the head voice is very pronounced, and preferable to that of the clear timbre, but the exaggeration of the same timbre dulls the voice and makes it cottony and hoarse.

*The timbres temper and correct each other by making the pharynx mechanically take that medium conformation between the two extremes which gives to any tone all the qualities which it should combine. We will concern ourselves with them particularly in the article on *The Emission of the Voice*.

The timbres, as we have just indicated them, are absolute in the same voice, relative in different voices.

CHAPTER IV

BREATHING [A]

One could not become a capable singer without possessing the art of the control of the breath.

The phenomenon of breathing is composed of a double action; the first is inspiration, the action by which the lungs draw in the exterior air; the second is expiration, which makes them return the air received.

In order to inhale freely, hold the chest erect, the shoulders back without stiffness, and the chest free. **Lower the diaphragm without jerking,** raise the chest by a slow and regular movement, *and set the hollow of the stomach.* From the moment when you begin these two movements the lungs will dilate until they are filled with air. [B]

This double procedure, on which I insist, enlarges the envelope of the lungs, first at the base, then by the circumference, and allows the lungs to complete all their expansion and to receive all the air which they can contain. To advise the abdominal breathing exclusively would be to voluntarily reduce by one half the element of strength most indispensable to the singer, the breath.

When the lungs are filled gradually and without jerking, they can retain the air for a long time without fatiguing. This slow and complete inhalation is what the Italians call a *respiro* [breath], as opposed to a light hurried inhalation, which gives the lungs only a little supplement of air for the need of the moment. That half-breath they call *mezzo-respiro*.

In neither case should the passage of the air through the throat be accompanied by any noise, under pain of spoiling the effect of the song and making the throat dry and stiff.

The mechanism of expiration is the opposite of that of inspiration. It consists of exerting a slow and gradual pressure on the lungs filled with air. Jerks, sudden movements of the chest [*coups de poitrine*], the precipitous fall of the ribs, and the abrupt relaxation of the diaphragm would let the air escape instantly.

*In fact, the lungs, spongy and inert masses, are enveloped in a kind of cone (the *thorax*), the base of which (the *diaphragm*)* **is a wide** and convex muscle arising from the edges of the chest **and separating the chest from the abdomen.** *A single fissure a few millimeters [*lignes*] in length (the *glottis*), placed at the summit of the cone, serves as a passage for the air. ⃞C

*In order that the air may enter the lungs, it is necessary that the sides [of the chest] separate and that the diaphragm lower; air then fills the lungs. If, in this situation, one allows the ribs to fall and the diaphragm to rise, the lungs, pressed from all sides like a sponge in the hand, immediately give up the air which they had inhaled. ⃞D

*It is necessary, then, to let the ribs fall and to relax the diaphragm only so much as it is necessary to nourish [*alimenter*] the tones.*

**One can, by subjecting the lungs to a special exercise, develop their elasticity and power to a very high degree. This exercise is composed of four different operations successively practiced:

1.   First, one inhales slowly and during the space of several seconds as much breath as the chest can contain;

2.   One exhales that air with the same slowness as with which it was inhaled;

3.   One fills the lungs and keeps them filled for the longest possible time;

4.   One exhales completely and leaves the chest empty as long as the physical powers will conveniently allow.

These four exercises, very fatiguing at first, should be practiced separately and at rather long intervals. The first two, namely the slow inhalations and exhalations, can be practiced more regularly if one will nearly close the mouth in such a manner that only a slight aperture is left for the passage of the air.

This is the physical means of obtaining the steadiness of the voice, about which more will be said later.

The breath, which holds the entire instrument under its subjection, exerts the greatest influence on the character of the performance and can make it calm [*posée*] or trembling, connected or detached, energetic or lifeless, expressive or devoid of expression.

CHAPTER V

THE EMISSION AND QUALITIES OF THE VOICE [A]

By this first study we prepare the tone, the basis of the talent of the student. The quality of the voice, we could not affirm too much, is the most precious element in singing. *My father often said that the beauty of the voice constituted ninety-nine percent of the commanding power [*puissance*] of a singer.* Now all uncultivated voices are, without exception, tainted with several faults, or less developed in certain regards than their usual good qualities may allow. Some voices are tremulous, others nasal, others guttural, veiled, harsh, shrill, etc., while many lack power, range, steadiness, elasticity, or mellowness. The teacher should not only correct these natural or acquired faults, and, while correcting them, prevent others from taking their places, but also discover and develop, among all the qualities of tone which the student's voice presents, that one which combines to the highest degree all the desirable conditions.

In order to correct the faults of the voice, as well as to perfect the quality of it, it is necessary to begin [*partir*] with this essential fact: that every modification produced in the timbre of a tone has its origin in an analogous variation in the interior position of the tube by which the voice is emitted. Each tint [*nuance*] of the tone which is emitted then represents to the ear the position in which one has held the tube. Since the differences in the tone correspond to the differences in that position, and since a flexible tube can gradually undergo an infinite number of modifications, it follows that the differences in tone are multiplied to infinity. It is from among all these tints that the student will choose that one which is most appropriate for each point in his voice. The tone which he should seek to adopt as preferable from the standpoint of instrumental beauty is that which is round, vibrant, and mellow; that is the important result which the teacher and student should seek together.

The other qualities of tone, useful in their place, will serve to express the emotions, and we will treat them in the article on *Style* [1872: *Expression*].

*The purest tone is obtained: (1) by flattening the tongue along its entire length, (2) by slightly raising the velum, (3) by separating the pillars at their base. Then the opening of the larynx is uncovered, and the pharynx reflects the sonorous column from the beginning in such a manner as to direct it toward the forward part of the palate. The voice, being reflected again by that part, which is firm and near the opening of the mouth, is emitted with ring [*éclat*] and roundness. The singer should then shape the instrument from the glottis to the lips by modifying the pharynx, the pillars, the arch of the palate, the tongue, the separation of the jaws and that of the lips in such a way as to direct the sonorous waves against the osseous part of the palate and to reflect them in the direction of the axis of the mouth, which amplifies the tone and is favorable to the emission of it. If the waves were turned back by an unfavorable arrangement of the reflector, the voice would lose its intensity and its purity. We could not recommend too much the extreme flexibility of the pharynx and supra-hyoidian area, because the elasticity and mellowness of the tone depend only on that flexibility. If the walls of the pharynx were rigid, or if the forward part of the neck were stiff, the tone would come out hard or choked. By teaching how one produces the guttural, nasal, harsh, etc., timbres, we have learned how to recognize them and avoid them.*

[B] **Numerous defects can alter the beauty of the voice. We will describe the most common ones and indicate the means of correcting them.**

Guttural timbre. When the tongue broadens at the base, it presses the epiglottis back onto the column of air, and the voice comes out as though squashed. One can verify this disposition of the tongue by pressing exteriorly a little above the larynx with the fingers. The tone, even under the pressure of the fingers, would not take on a guttural timbre if the tongue were not inflated at the base.

One easily sees what is necessary to correct the defectiveness of this timbre: the tongue, which is primarily charged, by its movements, with changing the voice into vowels, must be moved especially by its lateral edges, very little at its middle, not at all by its base. Let us add that the separation of the jaws should be approximately uniform for all the vowels.

Nasal timbre. When the velum is too relaxed, the voice can take on a nasal character, for the sonorous column of air goes directly to take its resonance in the nasal fossae before flowing out through the mouth. By pinching the nostrils, one can recognize whether the column of air, as soon as it leaves the larynx, is directed toward the nasal fossae before passing through the mouth, or whether it is directed immediately toward this latter cavity. It suffices to raise the velum to correct this fault.

Hollow [caverneux] *timbre.* [C] The tint of the voice will become muffled and hollow if one presents an obstacle to the sound waves. Thus, the tongue raised at the tip, or the excessive closure of the lips can produce this effect.

The swelling of the tonsils also can muffle the voice by acting as an obstacle. Young people often present the example of this temporary infirmity. It is accompanied in them by difficulty in forming and extending the head voice, a difficulty common to all women's voices in the state of fatigue.

Veiled tones. By teaching how to produce the veiled, cottony, dull timbre, we have learned how to recognize it and avoid it. We will add here only that the most intolerable of all the timbres is the clear timbre deprived of brilliance. At the same time we repeat that the dullness of the voice is corrected by pinching the glottis vigorously. The vowel [i] aids this movement of the organ.

1. THE MANNER OF PLACING [*DISPOSER*] THE MOUTH [D]

*The old masters attached a great importance to the manner in which their students placed the mouth. The tube for the discharge of the tones ending only at the lips, the best position of the tube would lose all its effect if the student placed his mouth badly. Opening the mouth in an oval form, like that of a fish, produces tones with a sad and grumbling character; advancing the lips in the form of a funnel gives a dull, barking voice; opening the mouth too much, which uncovers the teeth too much, makes the tone harsh [âpre]; closing the teeth too much makes grating tones. There is only one reasonable manner of moving the lips: that is to bring together or to separate the extremities of them. Since the separation of the teeth is invariable, it is evident that one can increase the outlet of the tone only by separating the corners of the mouth; in that case the lips are pressed against the teeth, and the voice gains from it perceptibly. If one would seek to obtain the increase by the retiring [éloignement] of the upper lip, one would produce, on the contrary, the bringing together of the corners, and consequently, one would lessen the opening of the mouth by rounding it. This position has the disadvantage of dulling the voice, of mixing the vowels into each other, of impeding the articulation, and of making the face hard, etc.

*Tosi[28] first, in 1723, and after him, Mancini,[29] tell us "that each singer should place his mouth as he habitually does it when he smiles naturally, that-is-to-say, in such a manner that the upper teeth

---

*28*Opinioni di cantori antiche e moderni.*

*29*Osservazione pratiche sopra il canto figurato.*

are separated perpendicularly and moderately from the lower ones."[30]

Let us go on to the study of tones.

2. THE STUDY OF TONES

The Stroke of the Glottis [Coup de la Glotte]. Hold the body straight, quiet, upright [*d'aplomb*] on the two legs, removed from any point of support;[31] open the mouth, not in the form of the oval O, but by letting the lower jaw fall away from the upper by its own weight, the corners of the mouth drawn back slightly, *not quite to the point of the smile.* This movement, which holds the lips softly pressed against the teeth, opens the mouth in the correct proportion and gives it an agreeable form. Hold the tongue relaxed and immobile (without lifting it either by its root or by its tip); finally, separate the base of the pillars and soften the entire throat. In this position, inhale *slowly and for a long time.* After you are thus prepared, and when the lungs are full of air, without stiffening either the *phonator* [1872: throat] or any part of the body, but calmly and easily, attack the tones very distinctly with a light stroke of the glottis on a very clear [a] vowel. That [a] will be taken well at the *bottom of the throat* [1872: right at the glottis], *in order that no obstacle may be opposed to the emission of the sound.* **In these conditions the tone should come out with

_____

*[30]Let us not confuse the more or less open position of the mouth with the smiling face [*physionomie riante*].*

[31]See *Breathing*. I have the arms held back in order to avoid impeding the action of the chest.

ring and with roundness.

      **One will take care not to slur the tones before arriving at the
correct intonation, which, furthermore, one should never seek with the
voice, but always approach boldly.**   *After an adequate preparation one
will attack the tone accurately, incisively, purely, and sonorously,
with the stroke of the glottis and on the vowel [a]. It is up to the
pharynx to position itself suitably by separating the pillars and by
lowering the velum.*

      **One must guard against confusing the stroke of the glottis with
the stroke of the chest [*coup de poitrine*], which resembles a cough, or
the effort of expelling something which is obstructing the throat. The
stroke of the chest causes the loss of a large portion of the breath,
and it makes the voice sound aspirated, stifled, and uncertain in intonation. The chest has no other function than to nourish the tones with
air, and it should not push them or shock [*heurter*] them.**

      It is necessary to prepare the stroke of the glottis by closing
it, which stops and momentarily accumulates some air in the passage;
then, much as a rupture operates as a means of relaxation, one opens it
with an incisive and vigorous stroke, similar to the action of the lips
in energetically pronouncing the consonant [p]. *This stroke of the
throat also resembles the action of the palatal arch performing the
movement necessary for the articulation of the consonant [k].*

      **Some teachers advise the use of the syllables [pa], [la], etc.,
in order to arrive at a precise attack. It seems to me that this means,
which moves the lips, tongue, etc., organs foreign to the emission of

the voice, has the disadvantage of masking the poor articulation of the glottis and can do nothing to rectify it.**

  Chest Register--Women's Voices. Women should practice first on the tones *b* and *c¹* [musical notation], which we choose as generally easy. If one knows how to attack the tone well, it should come out pure and sonorous. One will hold it only a short time and will repeat the attack several times. One will then go on to the half step above, and so on as far as *f¹* [musical notation]; then one will descend by semitones as low as possible without effort.

  The more one ascends above *d¹* [musical notation], the more it will be necessary to open the bottom of the throat. The vowel [a] must be as open as possible, without opening the mouth too much, which makes the tone gutteral (a trivial but established expression designates this tone by the epithet of *canard* [duck]).

  If a tone in the chest register refuses to come out **in the first attempts on the vowel [a], one will have recourse to the vowel [i], which brings about a more complete closure of the lips of the glottis and facilitates the emission of the chest tones. In order to obtain the tones which will come next, one will begin on a tone which one has mastered,** *and with the vowel [a]* one will make a vigorous portamento to the difficult tone. In order to establish that tone it will be necessary to control [*contenir*] it energetically. By proceeding from the known to the unknown, one will develop the chest voice *in the clear timbre.* It is understood that in this exercise, as well as in every other, one will be strict about the accuracy of the intonation.

One should insist on this first lesson, which is the basis of the teaching. I again recommend the stroke of the glottis as the only means of attacking the tones purely and without groping. When they are low, one should not attack them with force.

*One could not apply oneself too scrupulously to the observation of these precepts; the accuracy and the purity of the tones depend upon them.

It is necessary that the base of the tongue not swell and touch the arch of the palate; that position makes the voice gutteral and muf-fled. It is necessary also to avoid lifting the tip of the tongue if one wishes to maintain all the clarity of the tone.

The preceding observations extend to all the registers, to all vocalization.

Whether the voice is ready or not to ascend in the chest regis-ter, experience has taught me not to have it pass f^1 or $f\#^1$ in the course of the studies. *Later, when the student is very advanced, if she approaches the upper tones easily, one will be able to have her pass these limits in very vigorous phrases. I will give some examples of that in the section which discusses *Style*.*

Falsetto Register--Women's Voices. One will pass next to the study of the falsetto.

Sometimes it happens that the tones d^1 through f^1 [musical notation] are difficult to establish because of their extreme weakness; in that case, as above, it will be necessary to have recourse to a more easily available tone in the same register and arrive at the uncertain tone by very pronounced portamentos. One will neglect as useless all the tones below d^b [musical notation] .

The teacher will insist that the tones be emitted in pure falsetto and that one attack them by the stroke of the glottis.

The quality of the tones is rather often infantile; at other times it is veiled. One will correct the first of these faults by using the sombre timbre with the vowel [a], half [o]; one will combat the second with the clear timbre, using the very open [a] vowel [1872: the [i] vowel is recommended for this latter fault]. (c This register quickly exhuasts the breath; only time and practice can remedy that disadvantage.

Rather often the extreme notes [musical notation] of the falsetto are weak, while the tones [musical notation] , which are the first in the head

---

c) The unidentified translator of the Oliver Ditson edition of Part One suggests that the [a], half [o], in the above sentence is the [ɔ]. It could also be the [ɒ], which is the most sombre vowel of the true [a] vowel continuum.

register are round and pure. Since this roundness **and this purity**
proceed only from the position of the pharynx **and the contraction of
the glottis,** one will impart them to the preceding tones by arching
the velum **and by avoiding all loss of unused air.** It is thus by the
position which the pharynx adopts in the sombre timbre **and by the
pinching of the glottis** that these two registers are equalized.

Head Register--Women's Voices. The characteristic of the head
register is roundness. Sometimes this register is weak because of the
youth of the student; it is necessary, in that case, to wait for age to
strengthen the voice and to impart to it the fullness which it lacks.
At other times this weakness must be attributed to the student's lack of
skill; one must, in this case, make the same correction as stated earlier, which is to direct the voice toward the summit of the pharynx. In
no case should one sing past the g^2 ; the abuse of the high
tones has destroyed even more voices than age.

It is generally believed that high tones are lost because of not
being practiced; they should, on the contrary, be sung sparingly, even
by naturally very high voices.

Only when the throat has acquired some flexibility should one
seek to exceed the limits which we set now, but, in order to succeed in
it, one will never use sustained tones. It is necessary to try by means
of passages; it is always easier to reach, in the impulse of a roulade,
a tone which, attacked by itself, could not be produced, and it is thus

that one can attain, step by step, the final limits of the voice. It is necessary to proceed here with moderation and to give each new conquest time to solidify before attempting the next. The conformation of the throat must necessarily undergo, in proportion to our progress, some modifications which need time to become stable and natural.

Men's Voices. What we have just said regarding the three registers of the women's voices can be applied to the same registers of the men's voices, always paying regard to the observations which follow.

The bassos and the tenors will attack the tones in the same manner as the women. The bassos will begin in the chest register at the B or c [musical notation] and the tenors at the *d* or *e* [musical notation]. The tones [musical notation] in the basses and the [musical notation] in the tenors present a phenomenon worthy of attention. If one is not careful, it becomes very difficult to emit them in the clear timbre; the pharynx always tends to darken them. These tones, in this case, lack energy and ring; they become a source of trouble for the performer. It will be necessary then to struggle against this tendency and to make use of the only means which can consolidate that part of the vocal range: that is, to use the clear timbre while making the [a] **and [ε]** vowels more and more open. One must begin to round them slightly at the $a\flat$ [musical notation] for the basses, and at the *b* or c^1 [musical notation] for the tenors (the pure clear timbre would be too thin). One will continue to round (notice that I say to *round*, and not to darken) the tones b, c^1, and $c\#^1$

. Above d^1 the two timbres agree, but one should

not work on the sombre timbre in these last tones until one has mastered

them in the clear timbre, the most difficult to obtain in this part of

the range, and the only one which gives ring to the tones. If one

neglected this recommendation, one would be in danger of veiling or

choking his voice.

Between d^1 and $f\#^1$, tenors experience a great dif-

ficulty establishing firmly tones whose timbre is neither too shrill nor

too covered. We have added to the chapter on *messa di voce* [*sons filés*]

the explanations which we mean to give on this subject. Whatever the

ability of the singer may be, the tones in the

clear timbre appear shrill and recall the voice of the choir boy when it

is heard in a huge room; so, one should never use them except in the

sombre timbre. ⬛E

Tenors will not surpass the $f\#^1$ in the chest register

in the exercises. Most often they will begin the falsetto at the d^1

and will continue it up to the b^1 or c^2 .

A GENERAL TABLE FOR THE EMISSION OF TONES F

Each kind of voice will refrain from surpassing its own limits.

Contralto, Mezzo-Soprano, Soprano:

Basso and Baritone:

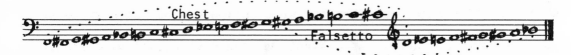

Tenor and Counter-Tenor:

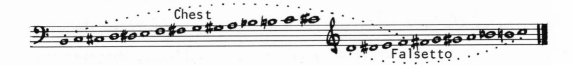

CHAPTER VI

BLENDING THE REGISTERS [A]

1. FEMALE VOICE

*As we have said, the chest register is generally denied or
rejected by teachers, not that one could not draw from its application
an immense advantage, nor that the suppression of the range which it
embraces would not deprive the singer of the most beautiful dramatic
effects or the most favorable contrasts, but because one can approach
the study of this register only with the help of profound knowledge,
under the threat of ruining the student's voice, and because the blending of this register with that of the falsetto can be secured only by a
long and ably directed labor. It has therefore been judged simpler and
more natural to free oneself from the difficulty of studying it.*

When the chest voice has been well established (which should be
done in a few days), the student must immediately work to blend that
register with the next. Sometimes nature herself has undertaken that
task, but voices thus favored are rare. This necessary study nearly
always disheartens the student, but it is up to the teacher to direct
capably and to take care of the voice which has been confided to him.
One will practice by passing alternately from one register to the other

on the tones  without interruption and without aspirat-

ing in that passage between registers. This succession should take place on the same breath; it should be practiced seldom and performed

slowly, firmly bringing out the passage, then the speed and the number

of repetitions can be increased. At one time the student should begin

with the chest register tone, at another with that of the falsetto. One

must not be afraid of accentuating the kind of hiccup which occurs in

the passage from one register to the other; only continued practice can

first alleviate it, then make it disappear.

The use of chest register tones will stop at f^1 .

*When one has acquired a certain facility, one will be able to

extend beyond the d^1 to the $f\#^1$.*

It is necessary to guard against reducing the brilliance and the

strength of the chest tones, just as it is necessary to give to the fal-

setto all the energy which it can tolerate. One is tempted to think

that it would be better to reduce the power of the strongest to the pro-

portion of the weakest. That is wrong; experience shows that the use of

such a procedure would have the result of impoverishing the voice. The

student will not give in to the tendency to aspirate the falsetto tones

at the moment when she leaves the chest register, whether she is prac-

ticing on two notes or on only one. I make the chest and falsetto reg-

isters coincide on the tones because it is necessary

to maintain the ability to change registers on each of these tones.

2. MALE VOICE

The rules which we have just set forth are as appropriate to the tenor voice as to the women's voices. If basses and baritones want to blend the chest and falsetto registers, they will do the same study, but a minor third lower.

SPECIAL EXERCISE FOR BLENDING THE CHEST AND FALSETTO REGISTERS [B]

[Translator's note: In the four exercises following, the notes with the stems going down will be sung in the chest register; those with the stems going up will be sung in the falsetto register. The exercises will be transposed upward by semitones as far as the last tone or pair of tones shown.]

CHAPTER VII

VOCALIZATION (*Agilità*)

To vocalize means to sing on vowels. We will curtail [*restrein-drons*] the use of the word vocalization with its indefinite meaning and replace it with the more precise words agility of the voice, and we will consider that ability under all its relationships. (d

Thus, to vocalize will mean for us: $\boxed{\text{A}}$

To perform with the voice, on all the vowels in turn:

In the two timbres;

In the three registers;

In the entire compass of the voice;

In all the degrees of force;

At all degrees of speed;

All kinds of passages:

By carrying them [*en les portant*];

By tying them [*en les liant*];

By marking them;

By making them staccato [*en les piquant*];

By aspirating them (a rare manner);

By marking all the different inflections;

By making stops in them;

---

d) In spite of his disclaimer of the term "vocalization," Garcia continued to use it nearly synonymously with the term "agility." We have generally translated it directly into English whenever he used it.

By combining all these means.[32]

These features of vocalization are closely tied to the manner in which the various parts of the vocal apparatus function: the breath, the vibrator, the resonator.

This very complex study not only has the advantage of furnishing the singer with all of the materials which he must use later; it is the only one which trains the organ to pass quickly and easily over all the pitches; it is the only one, as I have said, which equalizes the *compass* of the voice and makes all parts of the range familiar; finally, this study offers the only means of developing all of the upper extension of the voice without forcing the organ. [B]

1. PORTAMENTO (*Portamento di voce*)

To carry the voice is to lead from one tone to another by passing through all of the possible intermediate tones. The portamento can include from a half step to the greatest range of the voice. It takes its time from the last portion of the tone which it is leaving. The speed depends upon the movement of the passage to which it belongs.

It can go from weak to strong.

It can go from strong to weak.

It can be entirely weak or strong.

It can be performed in these different manners whether ascending or descending.

---

[32]Martini, in 1780, called, and not without reason, the varieties of coloration the *accents of the voice*.

The portamento will help to equalize the registers, the timbres, and the force of the voice.

*The voice will lightly touch the real note only by exaggerating the carrying [*port*] itself.*

The portamento should be performed with an equal and progressive movement. If one part of its scope were performed slowly and the others rapidly, or if the voice lowered its pitch before an ascending glide, the performance would have a detestable effect. In ascending portamentos, one should carefully avoid opening the vowel; it would almost be better to cover it slightly.

The scales--numbers 32 to 37--are excellent exercises to give the portamento boldness and quickness [*promptitude*].

We indicate it by this sign: ⌒

2. SLURRED VOCALIZATION (*Agilità di portamento*)

Slurred vocalization is a series of tones connected by portamentos.

In order to slur [*porter*] the tones, the air, fulfilling the functions of the bow on the string, will respond to a regular and continuous thrust, while the vibrator, for its part, undergoes progressive contractions or relaxations.

This style is rare; it is the last which one should study. It is necessary to guard against attacking the tones with a lower portamento. This fault is prevalent in France. One can combine [*rapprocher*] it with a stroke of the chest. This double habit destroys the most beautiful melody and revolts a man of taste. The slurred vocalization is repre-

sented by the same sign as the portamento: ⌒

3. SMOOTH VOCALIZATION (*Agilità legata e granita*)

To sing legato is to pass from one tone to another clearly, sud-

denly, spontaneously, without interrupting the flow of sound, or allow-

ing it to slur through any intermediate tones.

**Here, as in the slurred tones, the air must be submitted to a

regular and continuous thrust which joins all the tones together very

closely. The glottis alone can lend itself to all the instantaneous

changes, each of which corresponds to the frequency of vibration which

each different note requires.**

One can cite as an example the organ and the wind instruments,

which connect the tones without either slurring them or interrupting

them. This is the result which one must attain by the study of vocali-

zation. It forms the predominant quality of agility. The other styles

are subordinate to it and merely represent variations used to color it.

In order that smooth vocalization may combine all the character-

istics of perfection, it is necessary that the intonation be perfect and

that the value, force, and timbre of all the notes be perfectly even,

and, finally, that all the tones be connected to the same degree. One

can scarcely attain this end with less than a year and a half of dili-

gent study.

It is not always possible to obtain the smooth vocalization

directly, especially if the throat of the student has some very bad

58

tendencies, natural or acquired, which make the performance ponderous, cottony [*cotonneuse*], indistinct, or *gliding*. [C] One will combat these faults by making the vocalization marked (see *Marked Vocalization*). If, after two or three months of work, this means proves ineffective, it would be necessary to have recourse to the staccato (see *Staccato Vocalization*), then come back to the preceding, and then alternate them.

When the instrument has acquired a sufficient elasticity, one will again try the smooth vocalization.

If the performance is jerky or aspirated, as, for example, the

passage:[33]

then one is obliged to use the slurred vocalization to correct this new fault.

The *smooth vocalization* is the most frequently used of all; therefore, it needs no sign to indicate it, and students should always be on guard against *slurring*, *marking*, or singing in *staccato* any passages not so indicated.

4. MARKED VOCALIZATION (*Agilità martellata*)

To mark tones is to make them distinct by thrusting them, by

---

[33]The student will recognize that he is aspirating if, when holding a lighted candle in front of his mouth, he blows it out with his vocalization.

supporting each of them separately without detaching them or stopping
them. One will succeed in it by supposing that one has repeated the
vowel as many times as there are notes in the passage, *but without dis-
continuing the sound for breathing or anything else.* At the same time,
one will make a slight pressure with the stomach for each vowel; the
pharynx will experience a slight dilation for each tone. D Example:

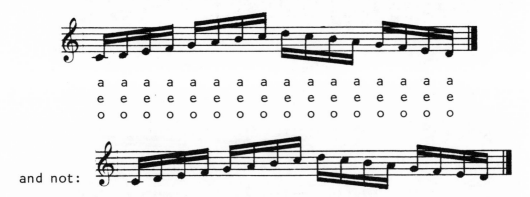

and not:

**But in this group of movements which each note requires--
namely, the changing contractions of the vibrator, the various impulses
of the air, the successive dilations of the pharynx--none should be
shocking or abrupt; no part of the passage should be interrupted by
breathing or by any other cause whatsoever.**

Marked vocalization has the double advantage of correcting the
habit of sliding between tones and of contributing to the emission of
the voice; bassos and dull voices have no better way of bringing out the
vocalization; it is, moreover, one of the principal resources for coloring passages. This style especially suits diatonic passages, and as a

60

consequence, roulades. It is up to the teacher to judge the moment when

he should mix this style alternately with the other. Later, one will

use the smooth and marked vocalizations as two distinct means which

should no longer have anything in common, except in descending scales,

where it is always suitable to slightly stress [*appuyer*] the final

tones.

One must beware of confusing the marked tones with strokes of the

chest. The first are produced by the impulse given to the first wave of

the tone to make its emission better without letting the least bit of

air escape before the waves begin; the strokes of the chest, on the

contrary, are only faulty aspirations which precede the tone and deprive

the attack of its purity; they cause the loss of breath and give songs

the appearance of a serious laugh, a combination both strange and intol-

erable.

Marked tones are indicated by dots and a tie:

5. STACCATO VOCALIZATION (*Agilità picchetata*)

Staccato tones are formed by attacking the tones individually by

a stroke of the glottis which detaches them from each other. (e If, in

---

e) The French, *piquée*, is sometimes translated as *detached*.

place of attacking them by the stroke of the glottis and leaving them instantly, one gives them a slight inflection which prolongs them, they are *fluted*, *echo-like*.

The first are indicated by dots, the second by apostrophes placed over the notes. Thus, the notes in the following example:

equal:

Besides the ring which they give to a piece when they are used with taste, they tend to give some elasticity to sluggish throats.

6. ASPIRATED VOCALIZATION

This is a rare style which will be discussed later in the section on *Repeated Notes* (see pages 142-143).

If it were possible to represent visually the different ways of performing a passage, we would do it thus:

Slurred Tones: Smooth Tones:

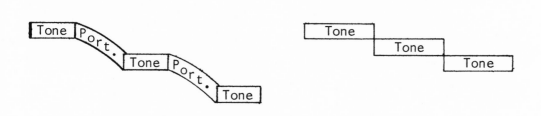

62

Marked Tones: Staccato Tones:

                                                > > >

**These five procedures, which the student should thoroughly possess, can be indicated by the following chart:

Portamento . . . .
{
Lungs . . *Equal* and continuous air pressure.
Glottis . *Gradual* changes of tension of the lips of the glottis.

Smooth Vocalization . .
{
Lungs . . *Equal* and continuous air pressure.
Glottis . *Sudden* changes of tension of the lips of the glottis.

Marked Vocalization . .
{
Lungs . . Continuous and *accented* air pressure.
Glottis . *Sudden* changes of tension of the lips of the glottis.

Staccato Vocalization .
{
Lungs . . Alternating pressures and pauses, corresponding to the
Glottis . alternating and sudden tensions and relaxations [*distensions*] of the glottis.

Aspirated Vocalization .
{
Lungs . . Continuous pressure.
Glottis . Alternating contractions and relaxations.**

EXERCISES FOR THE PORTAMENTO

Exercises 5 through 9 will be performed in two manners: first, as they are written; then, one will omit the rest in each measure and the portamento, so that the notes will follow each other up to the pause without interruption and without being slurred. The first exercise should be performed only as it is marked. (f

f) Because this paragraph appears in chapter eight of the sixth edition and is thus removed from all the vocal exercises (all exercises in that edition are in chapter nine), the "first exercise" to which Garcia refers is not clearly indicated. It may refer to the first exercise of the 1841 edition, which is actually the fourth exercise of the 1872 edition. Because that exercise is designed to blend the chest and falsetto registers, it should be practiced literally.

No. 6.

No. 7.

SCALES AND ROULADES (*Scale, Volate, Volatini*)

*Whoever would like to succeed in vocalizing the *roulade* without practicing first on two notes, then on three, etc., runs the risk of never being able to do any kind of passage well. On the pure execution of two notes depends that of three, four, five, and more. Therefore, it is necessary to apply oneself to it with the most scrupulous attention.*

Ascending agility is more difficult than *descending agility*. The voice slows down while ascending; while descending, on the contrary, it hurries. One will correct these defects by giving an equal force to all the tones, which should, moreover, be perfectly connected and distinct. *In No. 11 one will carefully avoid lowering the highest note and raising the lowest--a double danger to which we are exposed due to the natural tendency of the organ to shorten the distances.

Exercise No. 11 should not be dotted.

11. Slowly

The exercise which follows requires a special attention. When one repeats the same interval several times in a row, either the high note lowers, or the low note raises; often each of these notes tends to approach the other. **The major third in the exercise of the third and the leading tone in the exercise of the seventh (exercises 12 and 16) give rise to these observations.**

12. Slowly

It will be necessary to give strictly the same value to the descending notes as to the ascending notes; if not, it will happen in the repetition of the passage that the tones *f, e, d, c,* will be both sliding and hurried, and that, on the contrary, the tones *c, d, e, f,* will be slowed.

The leading tone is almost always flat, whether one is ascending or descending, if one does not carefully solidify the intonation.

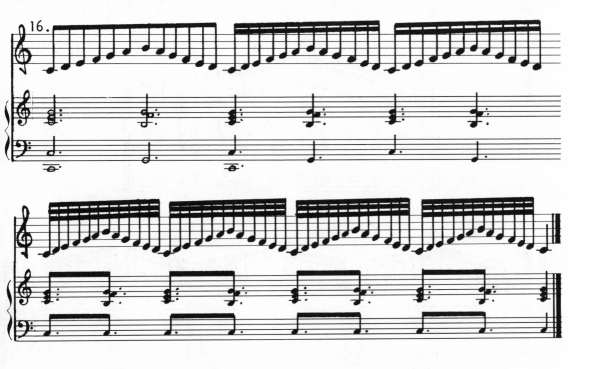

The semitone between the third and fourth degrees and that between the seventh and eighth degrees will be exact if one will be careful to raise the third and seventh degrees: that-is-to-say, the *mediant* and the *leading tone*. In these intonations, and especially on the seventh degree, one will sin less by excessive elevation than by lack of it. The contrary will take place on the fourth degree. When a

descending scale is out of tune, one can be assured that the semitones
are too large; that-is-to-say, that the third and seventh degrees are
too low.

If the first notes of a descending scale slip, they must be strengthened without widening the throat or swelling [*grossir*] the voice.[34] If the same thing happened to the last tones of the same scale, they should be sung more slowly, while intensifying and marking them (see page 58). One will make a pause on the next to the last note.

Example:  All the other

scales should be done the same way.

I advise here for the second time never to sing higher than the

notes . This interdiction applies even to all the exercises

which surpass these notes in their written form. It is necessary, as a result, to transpose those exercises into all the keys in which the

---

34Without separating the superior vocal tendons.**

voice will not be required to exceed this limit. Tenors and basses will
follow the instructions found on pages 47 and 48.

By indicating the last note of each scale to be as short as all
the others, we intend that it should be released instantly. If, while
studying the lessons, one has contracted the fault of dragging out the
last tones, making what one vulgarly calls *tails* [*queues*], this fault
will *infallibly* be reproduced in the pieces.

If one accelerates the tempo of scales whose first note is held, as in nos. 26, 30, 37, 38, etc., it is difficult to release that first note at the exact moment, and one nearly always exaggerates the value of it. **This fault slows the tempo of the scales, so it is necessary to set [*annoncer*] the tempo from the first note.** E

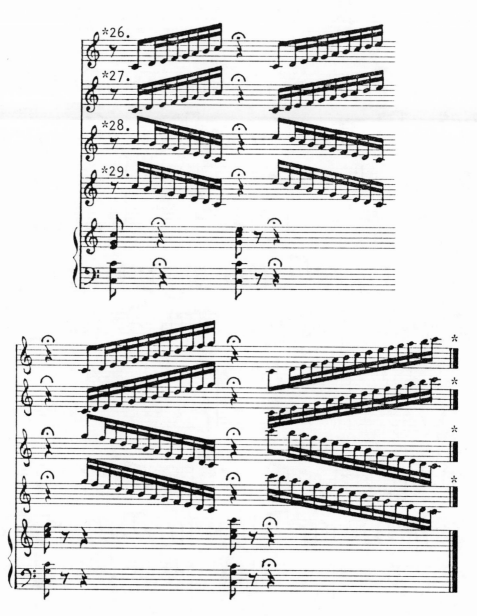

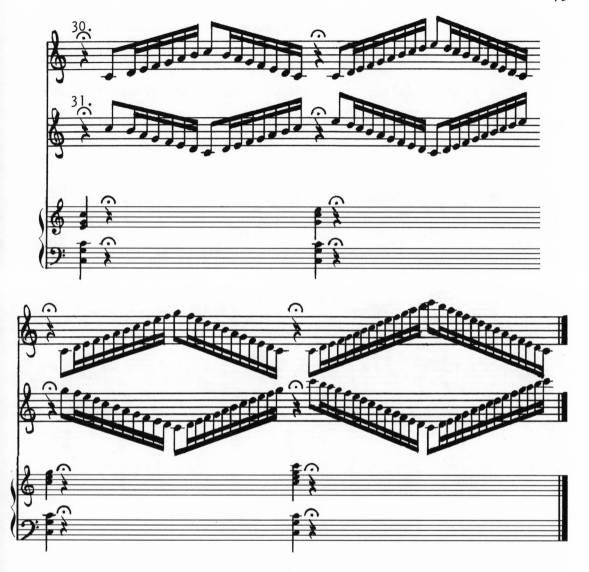

In the ascending intervals of the octave and the tenth, the upper tones are generally too low. In the same intervals, when descending, on the contrary, the lower tones are most often too high. *This last danger could be avoided if one would take care to make the throat supple; this condition would make the intonation easier and would also facilitate the passage from the falsetto register to the chest register in the clear timbre.*

76

One will sing all the scales slowly at first, breathing at intervals (see pages 10-12); then the increasing facility of the student will
permit him to increase the tempo and to breathe less frequently, and
finally, to perform the passages at full speed and on a single breath.

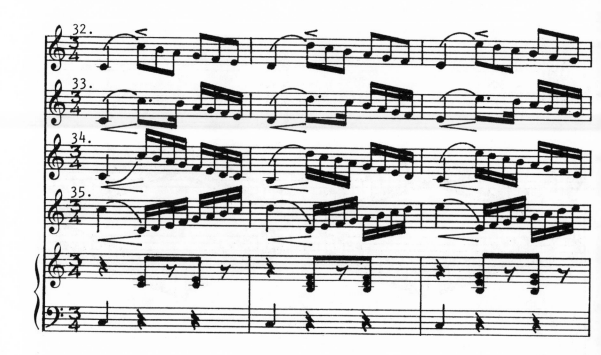

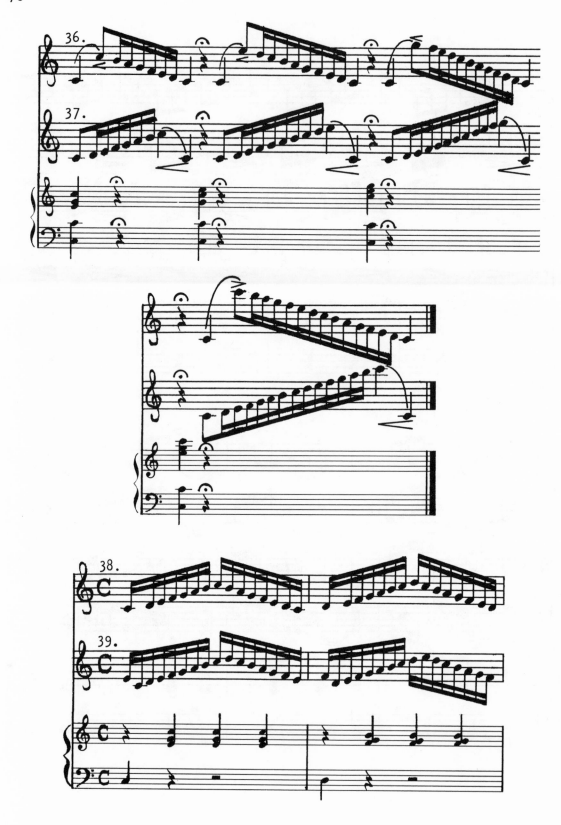

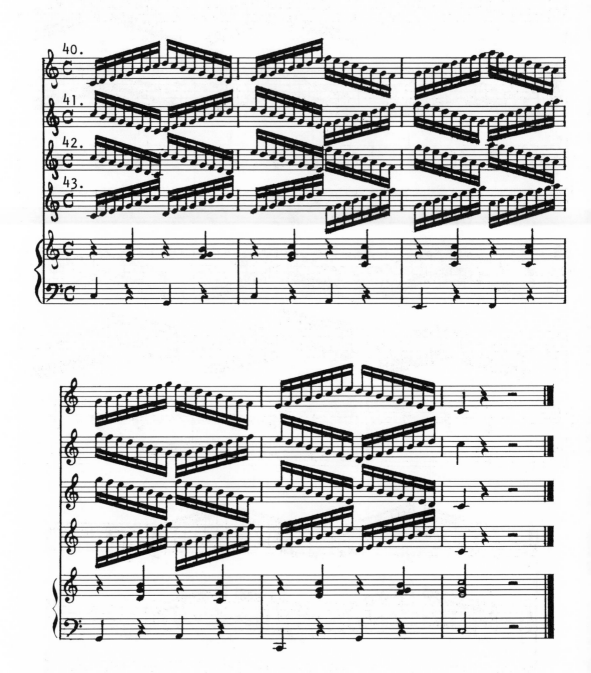

The exercises which follow will often present the passage from the chest register to that of the head, and *vice versa*. Instead of avoiding that passage, one must attack it boldly whenever it appears in the exercises. Although that separation of the registers is shocking at first, time and patience will make it disappear.

When one is able to sing the ascending and descending scales in a single breath, it will be necessary to omit the rests which separate them. In this case, one will be able to accompany each scale with a single chord.

The three notes of the triplets should be *equal in value*; in order to succeed in it, it is necessary to give an accent to the note which is slighted [*qui échappe*]. Generally it is the second. The character of the triplet also requires that one accent the first note.

Example:

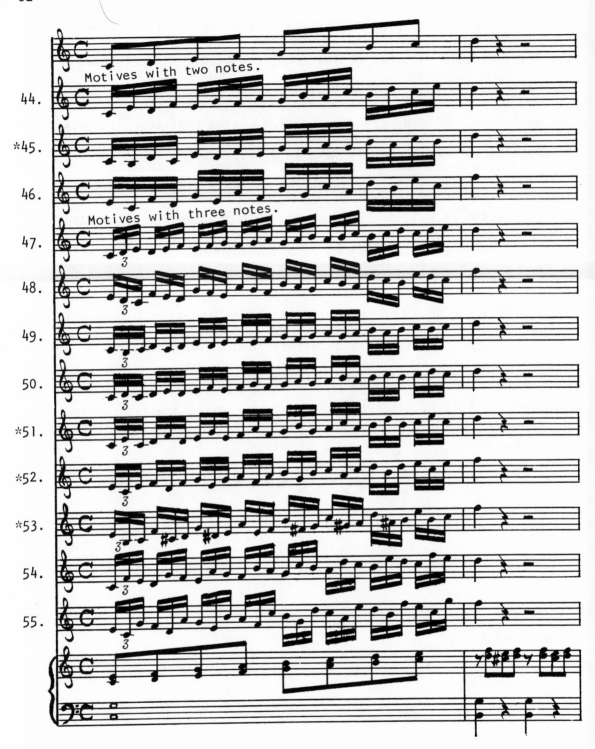

Exercise No. 52 and all those which likewise present the interval

of the *tritone*, comprised between the fourth and seventh degrees, merit

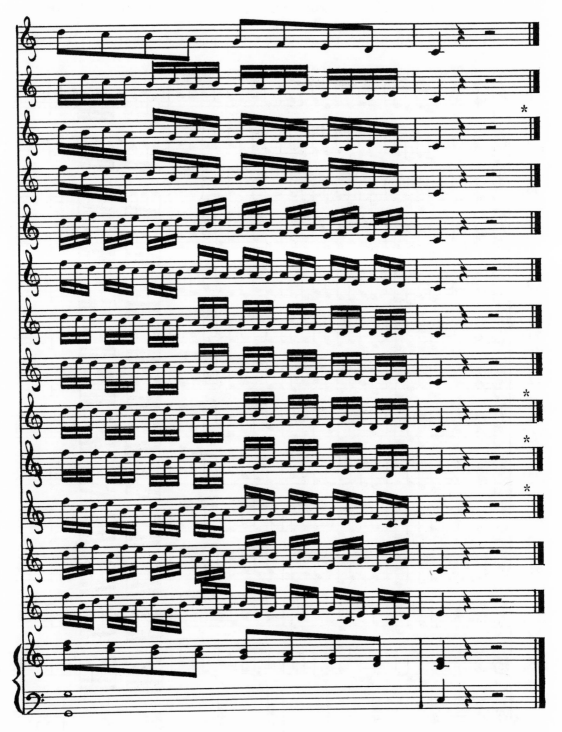

a special study. The three consecutive whole tones are hard to the ear, and one is always tempted to lower the augmented fourth by a semitone.

84

That lowering brings about a modulation which we want to avoid wherever
it is not marked, in order to accustom the pupil to that difficulty.   In

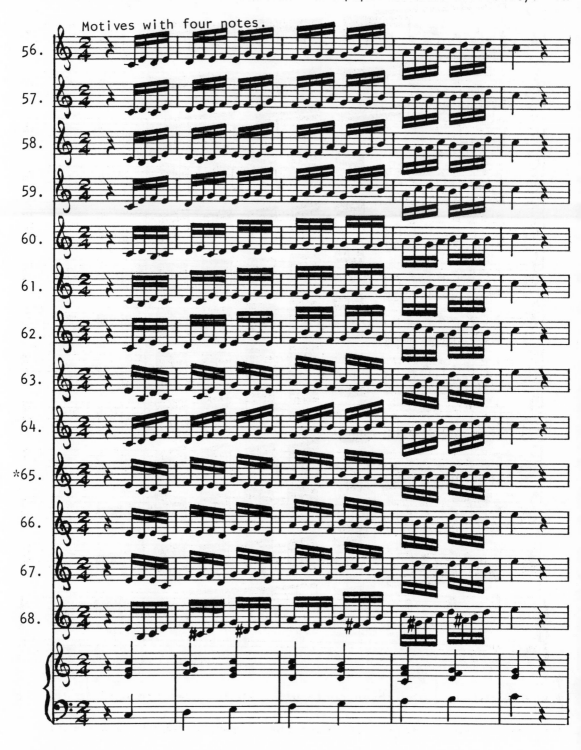

general, fourths and fifths are difficult to tune; thus, it is advisable to practice them.

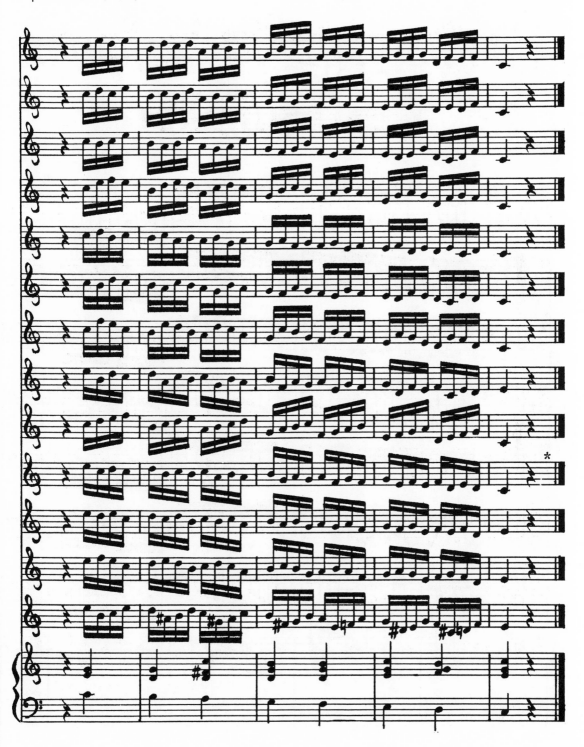

The student will also develop exercises from all the motives
indicated here. See pages 199 to 202.

The motives with six notes (sextuplets) are accentuated, not by groups of three notes, which would give them the character of triplets, but by groups of two or six notes. In general, to establish a rhythm in any manner whatever, it is necessary to accentuate the first note of the group.

88

108. Motives with eight notes.

94

*When the voice can be sustained unfailingly pure on the vowel [a], it will be time to exercise on the other vowels: [e], [ɛ], [o], [ɔ] (see *Pronunciation*, Part Two). The vowels [i] and [u] will be studied later, but only as much as will be necessary to accustom the voice to them.*

*156. Motives with twelve notes.

*157.

*158.

*159.

Motives with sixteen notes.

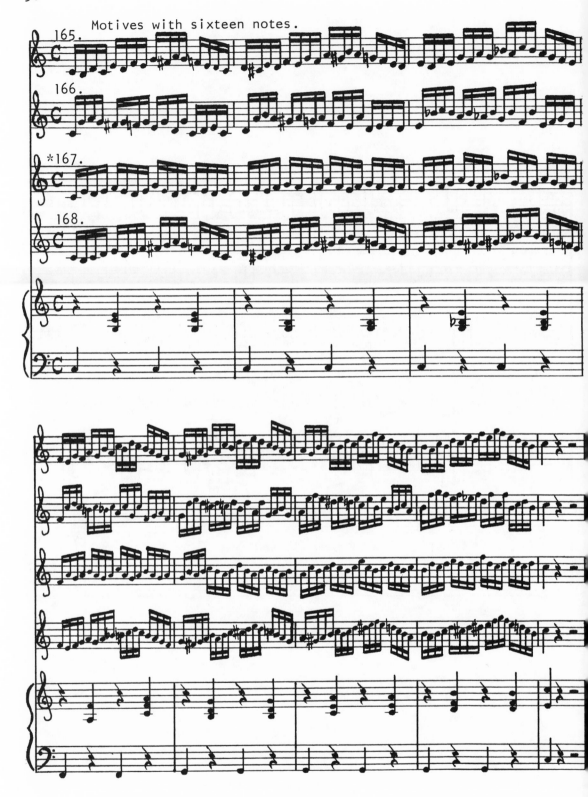

*The eight scales following (nos. 169-176) and their variations (nos. 177-184) are excellent exercises to make the throat supple and to give penetration [*mordant*] to the performance. We have already pointed

Motives with thirty-two notes.

out the tendency of the throat to shorten intervals; that tendency is

manifested here much more so because the same scale is repeated very

often.*

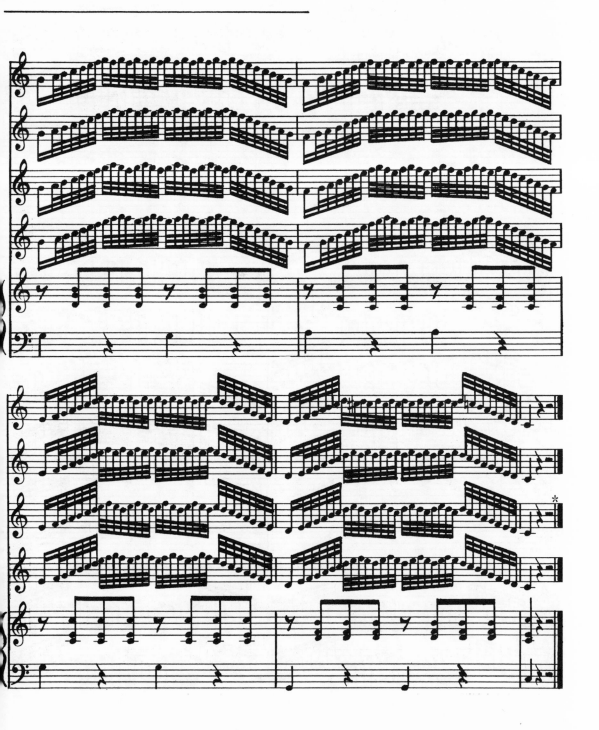

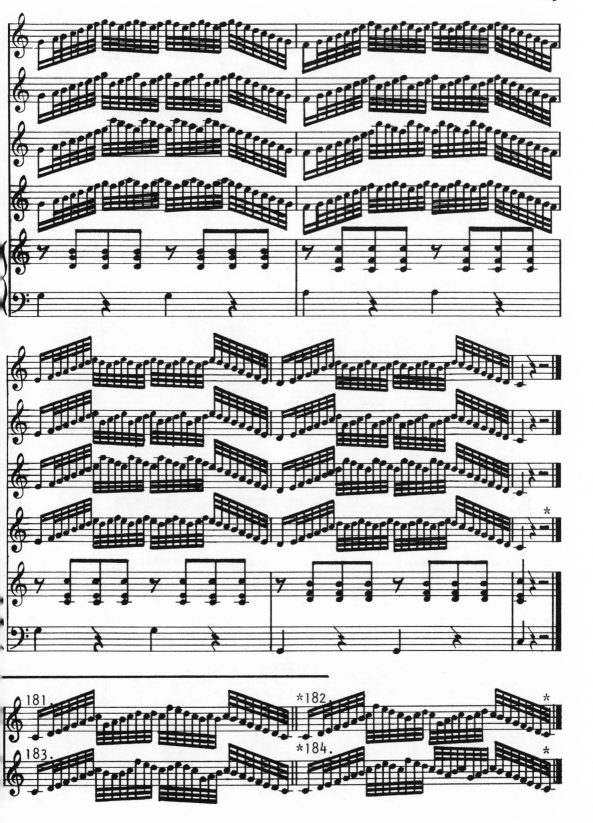

106

7. THE PAUSE [*Temps d'arrêt*]

The pause is a momentary prolongation of value given to a note taken at random in a passage composed of notes of equal value.

If, in the following examples, one wishes to make a pause on the notes marked by +,

these passages would be modified thus:

The pause, by giving a stress to the voice, permits the voice to make distinct what would have lacked clarity, and the passages gain much effect from it.

When one has succeeded in performing the preceding exercises with the Italian vowels, [a], [e], [ɛ], [o], [ɔ], at the tempo ♩ = 120 M.M., and maintaining the same value on all the notes, which will, moreover, be pure and perfectly clear, one will pass on to the nuances, to the inflections.

8.　INFLECTIONS

To inflect [*nuancer*] the passages is to vary the strength and tempo of them; thus, a passage purely vocalized with regard to the uniformity of timbre, equality of value and strength of the tones among themselves, will be uttered in the following sequence: first, as softly as possible, then a little more strongly, then moderately loudly, then loudly, and finally, in all the fullness of the tone, but *without violence*. Each exercise will pass through these five degrees of force.

We urge that the student sustain each tone at the same degree of intensity throughout its duration, carefully avoiding the fading of the tone as happens naturally. Example:

When the student has given a single and very even tint to all of an exercise (which is not easily accomplished), he will study breaking the tints; that-is-to-say, that the same exercise will be divided into equal or unequal groups of notes which will be vocalized alternately between *piano* and *forte*. One will divide and subdivide these groups more and more until finally ending by partial inflections.

These are a stress which one gives to a single note of a motive or of an exercise, all the others remaining equal and weaker. Each note of the passage should receive this inflection in its turn.

Partial inflections are indicated by placing on each note the sign >.

Examples of partial inflections which should be clearly marked are:

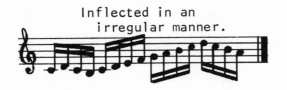

The student will tint the whole [*nuancera par masse*], that-is-to-say, he will *crescendo* and *diminuendo* and *vice versa* through the entire extent of the passage, only when he can tint it by inflections.

Examples of nuances of the whole [*nuances d'ensemble*]:

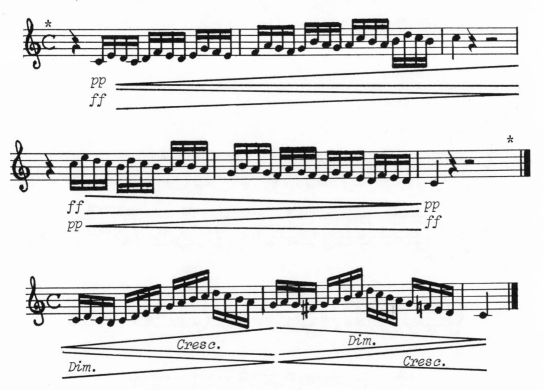

One will pass next to the staccato tones; that is, one will study in a staccato manner *all the exercises between no. 38 and no. 68* [1872: all the exercises of four, six, and eight notes].

One will again be able to combine tied tones and detached tones as we have seen done for the *piano* and *forte*, thus:

The *first* note of each pulse [*temps*] will be staccato, the other three tied.

The *second* note of each pulse will be staccato, the third, the fourth, and the first note of the following pulse tied.

The *third* note of each pulse will be staccato, the fourth, and the first and second notes of the following pulse tied.

The *fourth* note of each pulse will be staccato, the first, second, and third of the following pulse tied.

One will then be able to tie two notes and detach three, then tie three and detach three, and the same in all the possible combinations [1841: And the same with all the other patterns as well].

Examples:

When one ties by twos, threes, or fours, it is necessary to leave the second, third, or fourth note as soon as it has been touched, whether in ascending or in descending.

Ties and staccatos occupy all the means of the throat so much that it can rarely add inflections and marcatos to those nuances of the performance.

All these means or manners of uttering the passages, namely:

Portamentos;

Marcatos;

Ties;

Staccatos;

while applying to them all the vowels and their timbres:

Pauses;

Forte;

Pianissimo;

Fortissimo;

Piano;

Inflections;

Mezzo-forte;

and the various combinations of these means, form the inexhaustible depth in which the singer finds the brilliant resources which give life to his perfromance. We will apply ourselves to the use of these means in the article **_The Art of Phrasing_** [1841: in Part Two].

The alternating study of the exercises contained in the preceding paragraphs leads to the surmounting of the difficulties one by one. A single passage submitted to all these various procedures of performance will become the material for a long study and will change its features [_physionomie_] as many times as one submits it to different combinations.

The application of the method to follow in the choice and the distribution of these exercises requires long practice [_habitude_] and

112

much sagacity on the part of the teacher. One could not set out an invariable path in advance.

9. ARPEGGIOS

It is necessary in the arpeggios to pass with precision and firmness from one tone to another--whatever distance may separate them--neither detaching them nor slurring them [*les portant*], but connecting them spontaneously as on the piano. For that, it is necessary to stop [*éteindre*] each tone at the precise moment when one leaves it and to take the following tone by a light impulse; moreover, the position of the throat remains well fixed [*arrêtée*], free and natural, without relaxation or stiffness.

Proper arpeggios [*les arpèges droit*] will be thrust lightly; it is necessary to contract the throat a little while uttering them.

Motives with four notes.

Motives with six notes.

*198. Motives with six notes.

116

199. Motives with eight notes.

200.

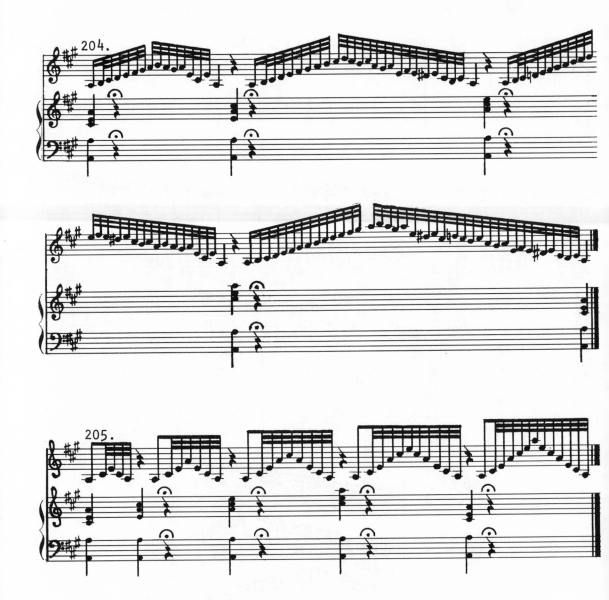

MINOR SCALES

CHROMATIC SCALES AND PASSAGES

If the irreproachable accuracy of each degree and the equality
and purity of the tones constitute the perfection of each passage of
agility, it is above all in chromatic scales and passages that these

characteristics are indispensable.

Chromatic passages and runs, being the most difficult to sing and to master, are for that very reason agreeable only when the series of notes is marked by so much accuracy and purity that one can recognize each of them successively [*compter successivement chacune d'elles*].

The division of any interval whatever into semitones requires at one and the same time a great assurance in the voice and an exquisite sense of intonation. If ever the memory of the intervals falters or the voice vacillates, the intervals become either too narrow or too wide. In the first case the performer will exceed, in the second, he will not attain the number of tones included in the distance which he must traverse; and, in either circumstance, the excess or the deficiency will have produced a detestable effect and the singer will have sung out of tune.

In order to acquire the necessary delicacy and assurance of intonation the student will study the chromatic exercises in a very moderate tempo; he will help himself by fixing in advance, in his mind, the first and last notes of the determined scale; then, dividing that scale by groups of two, three, or four notes, according to the need, he will count them mentally, having the first note of each group fall on the strong point [*frappé*] of each pulse.

The student will quicken the tempo only when he is secure at the slowest speed.

One will transpose these exercises, as the preceding ones, by half steps.

I think that one should, even in the pieces, avoid performing this kind of passage very quickly in order to leave the listeners time to comprehend it.

Because the chromatic scale relates to all the keys at the same time, the ear of the student is slow at first to recognize the relationship of the intervals [*intonations*], and if his voice were left to itself, it would lose its accuracy. Therefore, we will permit ourselves here to disregard momentarily the rule which prohibits us from doubling the voice with the piano. During the first attempts one will play the scale at the same time as the student sings it, and, to make this help effective, one will see that the instrument is perfectly in tune. But as soon as the student begins to pass judgement on his own performance, one will abandon his part to return to the usual accompaniment.

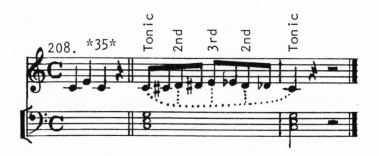

---

35 In a method recently published under the name of Mr. Lablache, one sees at the beginning of each chromatic scale an indication of the extreme points which it traverses. That indication having appeared good to us, we are reproducing it here. The student will abandon this means and the pauses which separate the ascending scale from the descending scale as soon as he has acquired the assurance necessary to undertake the two scales in a single breath.

10. THE SUSTAINING OF THE VOICE [*Tenue de la voix*] (g

The perfect agreement [*harmonie*] of the timbres, a controlled self-confidence, and the unvarying accuracy of the pitches constitute the breadth or sustaining [*tenue*] of the voice. This quality, the basis of a good style, is at the same time the most useful and the most rare. All those who push the voice by bursts or sudden gasps [*soubresauts*], who sing with strokes of the chest, who cut up the songs at the wrong moment, who leave and resume a timbre inopportunely [*hors du saison*], lack breadth.

These different **shortcomings** are connected to two principal causes:

1. The irregular expenditure of the air during the emission of the voice or the performance of a song; this irregularity produces jerks, thinness, and inequality of the tones.

2. The frequent variations of timbre which destroy the unity of

---

g) The term, *tenue de la voix*, is difficult to translate into modern English vocal usage. The unidentified translator of the Oliver Ditson printing of Part One rendered it as *Steadiness of Voice*. *The Art of Singing*, Part One (Boston: Oliver Ditson Company, n.d.), p. 33. The author's wife, Beata, translated a comparable section heading in the *Hints on Singing* by using the Italian term, *messa di voce*. *Hints on Singing*, trans. Beata Garcia (London: Ascherberg, Hopwood and Crew, Limited; New York: E. Schuberth and Company, 1894), p. 39. The term is obviously also related to what is frequently called "line." We interpreted it in that context in Part Two where it is related to holding a word or tone for its full value. We translated it there as "breadth." *A Complete Treatise on the Art of Singing*, Part Two, trans. Donald V. Paschke (New York: Da Capo Press, 1975), p. 27. It is rendered in the heading above as *The Sustaining of the Voice*, but the reader will note that in the ensuing paragraphs the term "breadth" is used wherever it seems to express more accurately the author's intent.

color and shock the ear.

The well sustained action of the breath and the mechanism of the pharynx, determined by the need of the passages and the unity of the timbre, are the physical conditions which assure breadth in singing-- the only ones which lead to an unshakable calmness and assurance in the pieces. The mechanism of the pharynx should be independent of the action of the chest.

11. SUSTAINED TONES

or THE PROLONGATION OF THE TONE DURING THE ENTIRE DURATION OF THE BREATH

The student, before undertaking the study of sustained tones, should sufficiently master the mechanism of the voice that he no longer need worry about groping aimlessly, and can hope for some progress at each new attempt. The study of these tones rests on the principles set down in the sections on *Breathing* and *The Sustaining of the Voice*.

Sustained tones come in four varieties:

Tones held with equal force;

Drawn out tones [*sons filés*];

Tones drawn out with inflections;

Repeated tones.

i. Tones held with equal force

As their name indicates, these tones are sustained with an unvarying intensity, whether one attacks them softly, moderately, or loudly.

ii. Drawn out tones (*messa di voce, spianata di voce*)

These tones begin pianissimo and grow in force by degrees until they reach the greatest intensity, which falls at exactly the halfway point of their duration; then, following a reverse path, the tone traverses the same scale, decreasing until, finally, it disappears.

One indicates drawn out tones by ⬦————⬦ .

It will be good to first divide this exercise. With one breath one will go from the pianissimo to the forte; then, with a second breath, from the forte to the pianissimo. This study, moreover, is completely as necessary as the preceding ⬦————⬦ .

The best teachers of singing formerly represented the *messa di voce* by means of the following example.[36]

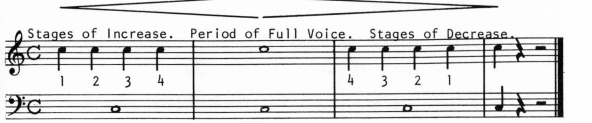

During the pianissimo, the pharynx will be reduced to its smallest dimensions, and it will dilate only in direct proportion to the intensity of the tone; then, in proportion to the weakening of the voice, it will return by degrees to its initial form. One must avoid raising or lowering the intonation while strengthening or diminishing the tones. These two tendencies are general. **It is necessary, in

---

[36] See Anna Maria Pellegrini Celloni, *Grammatica, o sieno regole di ben cantare*, Rome, 1810; *Second Edition, 1817.*

order to combat them, to use the system of compensation which we are going to set forth.[37] When the singer maintains his vocal cords in any state whatever, if he happens to push the air with more vigor, the pitch will rise against his will because the growing compression of the air increases the tension of the vocal cords and produces more rapid pulsations and explosions. It is easy to be assured of this fact. While one emits a tone, a sudden jolt to the region of the stomach suffices to force the voice to rise a second, a third, or more, and that rise, which results from the compression, like the compression, lasts only a moment. Consequently, in order for an intonation to remain invariably the same from the pianissimo to the fortissimo, *it is necessary that a voluntary relaxation* [détente] *of the vocal cords restore the intonation at each instant when it tends to rise.* The contrary will take place to return from the fortissimo to the pianissimo.**

As for the vowel, it should not be altered.

We recommend again not to attack the tone by scooping from below, nor by a stroke of the chest; one should begin it with clarity in the glottis. Upon releasing it, the student must not release what remains of the air by dropping the chest and relaxing the hollow [*creux*] of the stomach; the neglect of this precaution would produce a groaning in the last parts of the tone. **Neither will the student expect exhaustion to force him to abandon the tone. Mancini says somewhere: "Always keep in your possession a reserve of breath to end the tones easily."**

37See J. Mueller, *Physiologie du système nerveux*, translated by Jourdan.

One experiences a great difficulty *in drawing out the tones in both registers at the same time*, which takes place for women and tenors in this range:

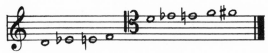

We know that, in order to pass from one timbre to the other on the same tone, it is only a question of alternating the mechanisms of the throat which produce them.

The student *will begin the tone softly in the falsetto and in the sombre timbre*. As we have seen, this procedure makes the larynx firm and contracts the pharynx. Then, *without varying the position, and, as a result, the timbre, one will pass into the chest register*, fixing the larynx more and more firmly in order to prevent making the abrupt movement which produces the hiccough at the moment of the separation of the two registers. Once established in the chest register, one will raise the larynx again and will dilate the pharynx to clarify the timbre in such a way that toward the middle of the duration of the tone it will have all its brilliance and all its force. In order to soften the tone, the student will do the reverse; that-is-to-say, that before passing into the falsetto register, *at the moment the voice is diminished he will darken the chest tone*, again fastening the larynx low and contracting the pharynx in order to support it and to avoid the jerk of the change of registers. Then he will pass slowly from the chest register to the falsetto; after which he will relax the pharynx and extinguish the tone. I deduce this rule from the physiological fact that the larynx, being held low by the sombre timbre, can produce the two registers without being displaced. Now, the displacement produces the hiccough which so disagreeably separates the one register from the other. **Here, as everywhere, one will attack the tones by a crisp [*sec*] stroke of the glottis; but *the energy of the attack will be proportional* to the degree of force which one wishes to impart to the tone.**

iii. Tones drawn out with inflections or with echos (*flautati*)

These consist of a series of loosely connected [*non discontinuée*] tones drawn out with different proportions, and as numerous [*multipliés*] as the extent of the breath permits.

One can arrange these inflections in different manners; they may be of equal duration and force,[38] or they may follow an increasing or a decreasing progression, etc. The great singers use them most commonly in the following manner: they first sustain a tone with a third of the breath; then, that tone is followed by another softer and shorter one; finally, comes a long series of echos, gradually weaker and closer together, the last of which can scarcely be heard. The throat must

---

[38]Some authors call this "making the voice vibrate" (*vibrar la voce*). M. Catruffo, in his method of vocalization, indicates this effect by means of syncopated rhythms.

contract and dilate with suppleness at each inflection.[39]

iv. Repeated tones [*martellement*]

Tones repeated while remaining on the same vowel are a kind of sustained tone; only in this case, the voice, without interruption, sub-divides by a series of percussions the note which would have been sustained in the first case.

Each of these percussions is articulated by one of the lowering and rising movements which the pharynx does in the trill. These movements are light and rapid; the tone should be caught again by a sort of **lower** appoggiatura of less than a quarter tone for each repetition. One will carefully avoid aspirating the different articulations of the same tone or performing them by a trembling or quivering of the voice; these percussions, being perceptible and charming only when produced by light voices, are suitable almost exclusively to women's voices. These percussions should not surpass four sixteenth notes for each pulse at ♩ = 100 on the metronome; their succession should always be soft and delicate to produce a good effect.

*Today people make the mistake of completely neglecting the study of repeated tones, used with success in the seventeenth and eighteenth

---

[39]Velluti expresses it: *"L'eco si fa flautato e per riuscirlo si ingrandisce tutto l'arco di dentro"* [the echo becomes flute-like, and in order to succeed in it the entire inner arch is enlarged].
Echoed tones are performed from weak to strong:

138

centuries.[40]

In our days, people are satisfied with the following repetition, the use of which has become trivial.[41]

---

*[40]Today, no singer, with the exception of Mme Damoreau, would be prepared to perform the following passage, although it is very simple.

Martini, in his *Melopée* (1790), explaining the various accents, calls the percussions with which we are concerned here: "a single tone tied and marked by strokes of the throat" [*une même note liée et marquée par coups de gosier*]; he adds: "One could also mark this tone with mordents." Here is the example which he gives:

And before him, in 1658, J. A. Herbst gives the following passage as an exercise:

See Joh. Andr. Herbst, *Musica moderna pratica*, Frankfurt, 1658.*

*[41]This repetition of the appoggiatura was introduced, according to the opinion of Lichtenthal, by Pacchiarotti. *"Si potrebbero chiamare,"* he says, *"appoggiature doppie, ed anche aspirate?"* [What could they be called, appoggiaturas doubled, and aspirated as well?]

EXERCISES FOR THE *MESSA DI VOCE* [*Sons filés*]

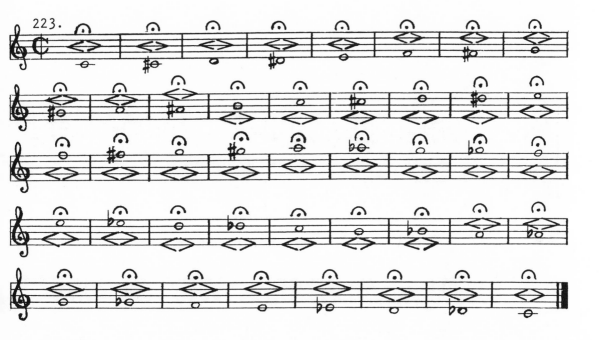

It is useless to study the *messa di voce* on tones which descend below c^1. There is never an occasion to use them in that manner. As for the tones above a^2, they are not more difficult, but more laborious to swell [*filer*] than the lower tones, and for that reason one would do well to neglect them until the need arises to use them in songs. The table above also furnishes material for the study of equally sustained tones and tones drawn out with inflections or echos.

*It will be necessary to restudy exercises 5, 6, 7, 8, 9, and 10,

and to do a *messa di voce* on each half note, followed by a slow and smooth *portamento*. The *messa di voce* combined with the *portamento* requires the greatest steadiness in the action of the chest.*

EXERCISES FOR REPEATED TONES

When the student must breathe, he will stop according to what was
said on pages 11-12.

There is another way of repeating tones; it is used only in rapid successions of notes repeated *one time each*. One can call it exceptional. It is what we have named *aspirated vocalization*. Examples:

The means of performing these passages consists of a slight aspiration placed before the repetition of each tone. This aspiration emanates from the glottis which allows a small particle of unvoiced air to escape between the repeated tones. This procedure leads to making them sufficiently distinct; whereas, in passages as rapid as those which concern us, if one used the method which we described above, the repetitions would be confused and unintelligible.

MORE EXERCISES FOR REPEATED TONES

146

[Note that these exercises are printed straight across page 147.]

12. APPOGGIATURAS AND LITTLE NOTES

Of all the ornaments of singing, the appoggiatura is the easiest to perform, and at the same time the most frequent and most necessary.

The appoggiatura, as its Italian name indicates, is a tone on which the voice leans. This tone is generally foreign to the harmony; it precedes and serves as a point from which to attack one of the real tones of the chord. *It can be above or below the chord tone; if it is above, one takes it as the scale offers it, whether by whole tone (see the place marked 1 in the first example below), or by half tone (see the places marked 2 below); if it is below, one nearly always does it by a half tone (see the places marked 3 below).* [F]

*Sometimes it is a tone within the harmony which functions as the appoggiatura, and then it can be separated from the tone to which it belongs by one of the intervals by which the chord is formed (see place marked 4 and 5 in the first example below).

*The appoggiatura can be given also by the simple delay of an actual tone of the harmony (see the places marked 6 in the examples below). This is the only case in which the appoggiatura is prepared; it was not prepared in the preceding situations [hypothèses]. Although generally indicated by a small note, the appoggiatura is always stressed more than the tone to which it belongs.

*The movement from the appoggiatura to the following tone takes place with clarity, connecting the voice without dragging it.

*Here are some examples which combine the different appoggiaturas about which we have just spoken:

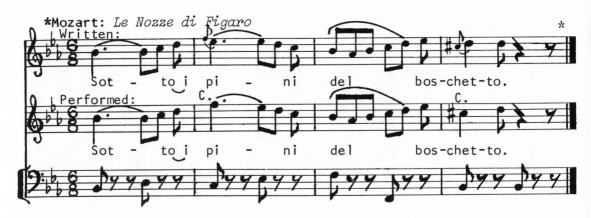

*The duration of the appoggiatura is very flexible. If the measure is even, the appoggiatura assumes one half of the value of the tone which it is intended to embellish (see the places marked A in the examples above).

*If the principal note is dotted, or if the measure is uneven, the appoggiatura borrows two thirds of the value of the principal tone (see the places marked B in the examples above).

*The appoggiatura absorbs the entire value of the principal tone when the duration of the latter is prolonged by a tie [liaison] (see the places marked C in the examples above).

*Finally, the appoggiatura can be extremely rapid (see the place marked 4 in the first example above).

The requirements of the situation and the nature of the melody will determine the choice from these different applications more surely than any precepts could do it.

Among the appoggiaturas it is necessary to distinguish the acciaccatura. This is a lively little note which precedes, at a distance of a whole tone or a semitone, a second note as short as itself.

The voice abruptly precipitates these two notes, so to speak, and stops only on the third. Examples:

The method of performance presented in the last example would remove from the *acciaccatura* the lively and resolute [*décidé*] character which distinguishes it in order to give it that of triplets.

Appoggiaturas can be simple or double. There is no reason to practice the first separately. Their physical performance presents no difficulty. It will suffice to study them in the pieces; the art consists in learning their nuances and using them with taste.

The Turn (Fr., *Mordant*; It., *Gruppetto*)

Among the various combinations presented by the double appoggiaturas, it is necessary to distinguish those which are formed by two or three descending and ascending notes. Examples:

Some authors name the first two examples *mezzi gruppetti*; the two others are always called *gruppetti* and are indicated by the sign ∿.

*Fr. Domingo Varellas de San-José and Johan Samuel Petris

designate the two contrary turns by the reversal of the same sign.[42]

Example:*

All the other combinations of appoggiaturas, such as

fall within the domain of double appoggiaturas or little notes (see exercises 260-275 on pages 184-186).

The *gruppetto* is, after the appoggiatura, the most commonly used ornament, and for that very reason, the most necessary in singing. As it is composed uniquely by the combination of the lower and upper appoggiaturas of the principal note, one should apply to it the rule established for the appoggiaturas which prescribes always placing an interval of a semitone between the little note below and the large note; from that it follows, as the *Method* of singing of the Conservatoire observes, that the *gruppetto* cannot exceed a minor third without losing some of its grace and lightness.

One should secure [*obtenir*] the *gruppetto* by a *sforzando* on the first of the three tones which comprise it, attacking it freely, with boldness, in such a manner that it is distinguished over the tone which precedes it and that which follows it. The effort given to that tone should carry along the other two in their turn. One will study it

---

*[42]Fr. Domingo Varellas de San-José, *Compendio de musica teorica e pratica* (Porto, 1806), in 4°. Johan Samuel Petris, *Introduction à la Musique pratique* (Lauban, 1767).*

slowly at first in order to establish the proportions, the clarity, and the intonation; then one will gradually increase the speed.

The *gruppetto* can occupy three different places relative to the tone which it is intended to ornament.

It can, first, attack the tone; second, occupy the middle of it; and third, end it. In the first case, one should assign to it the first instant of the value of the tone. Examples:

In the second case, one will first establish the tone, and, in the middle of its duration, one will perform the turn. Examples:

In the third case, one will complete the value of the note with the turn. Examples:

Cimarosa: *Il Matrimonio Segreto*

Since the unique character of the turn is to be quick and crisp [*incisif*], one should confine it into the duration of a sixteenth note at the value of ♪ = 100 M.M. Placed over any note whatever of exercises 56-148 on pages 84-92, it will take only the value of the sixteenth note or the value of three sixty-fourth notes.

In these exercises all the tones should be sung softly, with the exception of the three which form the turn.

EXERCISES FOR THE TURN

The turn at the beginning:

The turn in the middle:

The turn at the end:

Application of the Turn to Exercise 69

The forms of the turn which follow are called *battuta di gola* [strokes of the throat].

EXERCISES FOR THE ACCIACATURA

13. THE TRILL

The trill is an alternating, striking [*martelée*], rapid, and

equal succession of two contiguous tones at an interval of a semitone or a whole tone.*43* It is indicated by the letters *tr*. When this sign is

placed on a note, it signifies that the trill should be composed of that

note and the note a semitone or a whole tone above, according to the key

[*l'accord*]. The note which bears the trill sign is called the principal

note, and it is never combined in a trilled succession with the lower

tones. The upper note is called the auxilliary note.

**In addition to these two notes there is a third which is at an

interval of a semitone or a whole tone below the principal note and

which should be called the note of preparation or of termination, since

it fulfils both these functions; but the trill is always begun and ended

by the principal note.**

The trill is only a regular oscillation from low to high and *vice

versa* which the larynx receives.**44** This convulsive oscillation

takes its birth in the pharynx by a very similar oscillation of the

muscles of that organ. Old people whose voices are unsteady offer us an

example of an involuntary trill. In their case the trill is irregular

because of weakness; in the case of younger subjects it should become

---

*43*Il primo che rinnovo nel canto il trillo, incognito affato
alle voci dei cantori dei due secoli 15 e 16, fu Gian Luca Conforti, di
Mileto in Calabria, agragato* [sic] *nel collegio dei cantori ponteficii
il 4 nov. 1591.* (The first to revive the trill, quite unknown to the
voices of fifteenth and sixteenth century singers, to singing was Gian
Luca Conforti, from Mileto in Calabria, admitted into the College of
Papal Singers November 4, 1591.) He *revived* the trill, since it was
known to the ancients under the names of *vibrissare, vibrare,* as wit-
nessed by Pompius Festus and Pliny the Elder [*Pline le naturaliste*]
(Baini, *Memori della vita di P. de Palestrina).**

**44The English call the trill *shake*; this word, which means
trembling, seems to me very appropriate.**

regular through flexibility. We are going to apply ourselves to the mechanical act which will give us the desired acoustical result.

It is necessary to impart to the larynx a regular oscillatory up and down movement, similar to that of the piston working in the body of a pump, taking place in the pharynx, *which serves as an envelope for the larynx.*[45]   *One would not know how to make the pharynx too supple in order that the shortening and lengthening of the depressor and elevator muscles may take place with ease and rapidity. One will have an approximate idea of this operation if one suddenly and rapidly, while holding the mouth open, makes the movements of swallowing; in this case the base of the tongue fills the principal function. In the trill the point of action is placed elsewhere, and the tongue yields to the agitation which is transmitted to it.*   These movements, appreciable to the touch, are more or less visible [s'annoncent] on the exterior in proportion to the fleshiness of the neck.

Nightingales offer a striking example of the phenomenon which we have just described.

People have generally adopted the presumption that the trill is a

---

[45]One can obtain a factitious trill by agitating the throat exteriorly with the fingers. We give this fact as a proof of the accuracy of our description.

The succession of the trill is the most rapid of all the vocalizations, but so rapid that between the speed of $\quad$ = 152 M.M., the fastest speed that the voice can vocalize, and that of the speed of the

trill, $\quad$ = 200 M.M., there is a wide gap. One can thus establish this convulsive trembling as the highest possible speed in vocalization.

gift of nature and that the voice which nature has deprived of it should

not attempt it. Nothing is more erroneous than that opinion.*46*

The trill does not result from two notes struck one after the

other and accelerated to the greatest rapidity, as for example:

This passage will never be anything but an agility passage which

can precede or follow the trill; it is a variety of the trill which is

called the *soft trill* [*trillo molle*] when it is placed as follows:

Rossini: *Il Barbiere di Siviglia*

The more equal and free that these regular movements are, the

more accurate the intervals of the trill are.

The voice thus shaken in an interval of a second passes through

all the intermediary tones; but, as it regularly confines its excursions

---

*46*I cite as an example Madame Pasta. The voice of that celebrated singer was harsh and veiled. A natural difficulty had never permitted her, in spite of the most obstinate study, to approach the trill
or to perform ascending roulades in a quick tempo; her performance con-
sisted of descending scales and broken runs. Ascending scales remained
an invincible difficulty for her; but it was not the same with the trill
when she finally succeeded in mastering the mechanism of it. In fact,
Madame Pasta (on November 15, 1830), after ten years of a brilliant
career, was heard to emit at the Bouffes one of the most magnificent
trills with inflections in the aria from *Tancredi* that the dilettanti
could remember. She placed it at the organ point which precedes the
reprise of the motive: *Saro felice.**

between two invariable limits, these two extreme points attract all the attention.

The reader should already understand that the more compass [*éten- due*] one gives to the oscillations of the larynx the more distance the trill will take in. Thus, one can carry it to a semitone, to a tone, to a minor third, a major third, a fourth, a fifth, etc. This will sur- prise, perhaps, for it is not customary to have a trill surpass a major second. The use of such ornaments would undoubtedly be in poor taste, and I do not approve of applying them in pieces; however, I advise the study of them, but only until one understands the oscillatory movement. It is true, we cannot seize upon each one of these movements in particu- lar, but we can excite them **and stop them** at will, then fix the lim- its of their range and maintain their perfect isochroneity. Sometimes from the first attempt one will make himself the master of this move- ment; a few months of study should suffice for every gifted student with ordinary aptitude.

In nearly all methods of singing, and notably in that of Martini, after him in that of the Conservatory, and still later, finally, in a great number of others, one is advised to study the trill by dotting the principal note.

*Example from Martini:

*Example from the Method of the Conservatory

Messa
di voce.

Comparing this procedure with the very essence of the trill and the application of it which all the good singers have always made, we cannot refrain from declaring it radically bad. **I urge students to seek the trill through the spontaneous trembling of the throat, and not through the progressive movement of the two notes.**

One will do well to practice first within the limits of this

octave,

the range of which requires less contraction than the higher tones. When the movement of the trill is broad and easy, it will be necessary to immediately regularize the form of it.

The major or minor trill, if one accounts for all the different manners by which the celebrated singers have always used it, offers the following varieties:

Either it can belong to a single tone, or it can be used in the body of a phrase in a *measured succession*; if the trill is isolated, it can take the character of the *trillo mordente* (trill with a turn), the *trillo radoppiato* (redoubled trill), or, finally, the *trillo lento* or *trillo molle* (slow or soft trill). If it is used in a measured succession, one can use it either in a *succession of disjunct intervals*, or in a *diatonic scale*, or in a *chromatic scale*, or, finally, in the *portamento.*

i. The isolated trill, major or minor

If the trill is free, as one sees in organ points, or if, being measured, it has a sufficient value, all the good singers attack it and leave it by a regular preparation and termination which make the effect of it very pleasant. The preparation consists of having the two tones which comprise the trill preceded by a tone which is a semitone or a whole tone below the principal tone. Those two tones, by a gradual but short acceleration, lead to the effect of the oscillation. The trill so begun is developed following the rules for sustained tones or the *messa di voce* (see pages 133-139). The termination is done softly, as is the preparation, and consists in placing immediately after the abruptly stopped trill the note below the principal note, which is itself fol- lowed by a final note or by a final passage. Example:

This preparation and these terminations are the most simple; one can vary them infinitely; we give several examples of these combinations on pages 176-179.

The pupil should remain free [*rester maître*] to stop the trill according to his own taste, and he will invariably stop it on the principal note; without particular attention he would not be able to stop the oscillation imparted to the throat at the right time.

ii. The trill in a diatonic progression

When trills are placed in the body of a phrase in measured succession, ascending or descending, one generally does not prepare them at all because one usually does not have the time to do so. Then one attacks them abruptly by the upper note, and only the final trill receives a termination. Example: G

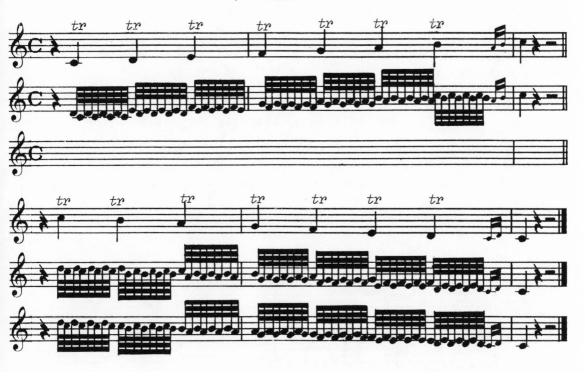

One must choose, in our opinion, between the two manners shown in

the descending progression.

One should omit the termination of each trill only if there is no time to perform it; besides, the termination enlivens the effect.

iii. The trill in a succession of disjunct intervals

One attacks the trills by the upper appoggiatura when the succession is made by disjunct intervals; but then each trill receives its termination. Examples:

It is through these forms that the throat is familiarized most rapidly with the difficulties of the trill and is led to all the other forms which we are going to discuss. They took their birth in the different applications of the isolated or measured trill which have been made by skilled singers.

iv. The trill in a chromatic succession

The chromatic trill, whether ascending or descending, is attacked equally by its upper tone with intervals of a semitone or a whole tone, according to the tonality of the phrase in which one performs it. Example:

v. The trilled portamento

This trill can be applied to the portamento, whether ascending or descending. Tosi, who was the first, to my knowledge, to speak of this kind of trill, says that one achieves it by imperceptibly raising or lowering the voice from one longer tone [*comma*] to another with a continuous trill in such a manner that the listener cannot distinguish the degrees of the rise or fall of the pitch.

In this case the portamento is very slow.

vi. The trill mordent [*trillo mordente*]

This is attacked more rapidly than the other kinds of trills, but it ceases immediately after the attack; its duration, like that of the turn [*mordant*], is instantaneous; it is indicated by the sign ᴧᴧ.

After Tosi, the abbe Lacassagne, in 1766, and still later the method of the Conservatory, and many others have notated this trill in approximately the same manner while describing it under the different names of shake [*tremblement*], trill mordent [*martellement*], thrown [*jeté*] cadence or trill, shortened [*tronqué*] trill, etc. Examples:

Among these diverse forms the last is the most exact and the most secure [*sur*]. This one is the most brilliant:

The well performed trill mordent will lead to the double trill.

vii. The double trill [*trille redoublé, trillo raddoppiato*]

It is again from Tosi that we borrow the definition of this trill. One obtains it by inserting some tones into the middle of the

major or minor trill. These tones suffice to form different trills from
a single one. When purely performed by a pleasant voice, this ornament
has a beautiful effect, especially when the alternating interruptions
are produced by strongly articulated tones. This trill is particularly
suitable to the head tones of the female voice. It is indicated by the
sign ᴧᴨᴠ. Example:

viii. The slow, or soft trill

This is the least important of all; we spoke of it on page 161.

ix. The faults of the trill

The principal faults of the trill result from the inequality of
the oscillations. That inequality often makes it halting [boiteux] and
dotted; it can make it encompass the exorbitant range of a third or a
fourth; sometimes, on the contrary, it can enclose it in the second
below the principal tone instead of the second above, or make it end on
a different interval from that where it began; other times the second
above is minor when it should be major. Also often, the oscillatory
movements are replaced by a kind of ridiculous neighing **produced by
the smallness and the stiffness of the trembling,** known by the names

aprino [wild goat trill] or *trillo cavallino* [horse trill].

The trill, the appoggiatura, the gruppetto, and their various manners of performance are only described here; it is in the second part of this work that these topics receive their full development.

EXERCISES FOR THE MEASURED TRILL

The appoggiatura which attacks the trill should stand out above all the other tones.

The student will sometimes need to suppress, sometimes retain the termination.

EXERCISE FOR THE TRILL MORDENT

EXERCISES FOR THE CHROMATIC TRILL

Before trying the chromatic trill, repeat the chromatic scale to which it is related several times; that is the way to fix in your memory the delicate and difficult intonations through which one must pass.

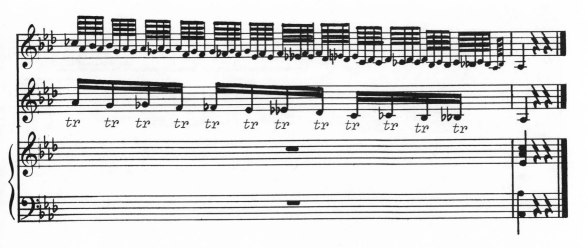

The pupil, after having studied each half of a given exercise separately, will be able to try combining them in a single breath. The last exercise, thus performed, would be a veritable *tour de force*, an example of which has been given to us only by the Chevalier Balthasar Ferri. That singer flourished about 1660 (see *l'Istoria musica* by Angelini Bontempi).

EXAMPLES OF THE PREPARATION AND TERMINATION OF THE FREE TRILL

The pupil who has arrived at this point will have acquired enough strength to attempt combining the trill with the *messa di voce* or with some other kind of passage which prepares it. For that he will calculate the length of his breath in such a manner that he will be able to develop equally the trill and the *messa di voce* or other passage which precedes it.

254 (cont.).

Here are several examples of preparations of trills as they were used in final cadences of seventeenth century sacred music (see Herbst).

EXERCISES FOR THE HALF BREATH

h) The B. Schott's Sohnen
edition shows the second half
of this measure as follows:

As one can see, the first c^2 and both f^2's were sharped in the original, breaking the diatonic sequence pattern so customary throughout Garcia's method. We deemed it proper to make the above alterations to restore that diatonic sequence.

LITTLE NOTES [H]

When several small notes are used together to attack a single
tone, one performs them quickly, clearly, and with brilliance.

EXERCISES ON THE MAJOR NINTH CHORD

188

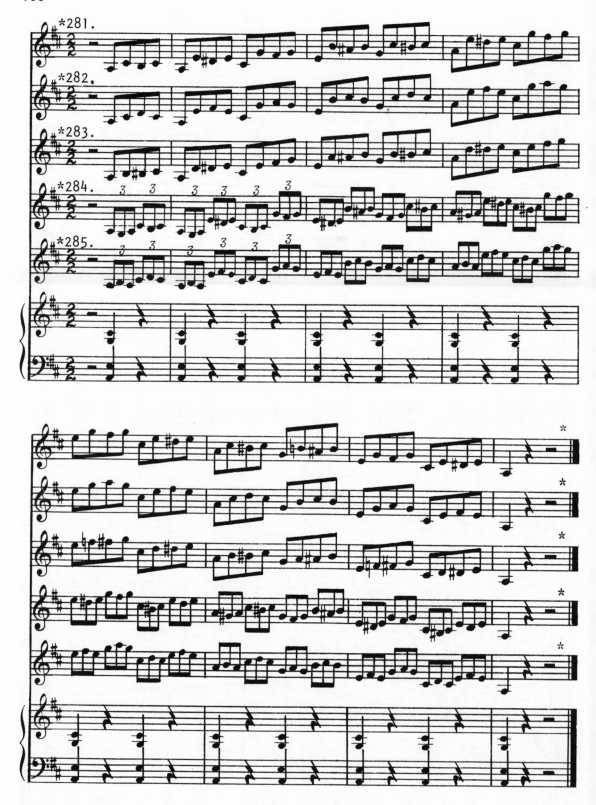

192

*The theme which we have established on the major ninth chord to
serve as the basis of the preceding exercises can undergo a large number
of modifications; the simplest of them are obtained by a change of
accent; that-is-to-say, by tying the notes of the original passage by
twos, by threes, etc., by applying inflections to them (see pages 106-
112), by ornamenting them with lower or upper appoggiaturas, by gruppetti, by the trill, etc. These various means provide us with the following exercises:*

194

The student will develop the following patterns, placing them in a key which is suitable for his voice.

A SUMMARY OF AGILITY

It would be impossible to record all the modifications of the mechanism of agility; only experience can teach them. Nevertheless, one can set forth these fundamental considerations, based upon the expenditure of the air and the action of the pharynx.

When the agility is performed pianissimo, it is necessary to hold back the exhalation, and to expend only a thin stream [*un filet*] of air. The pharynx, narrowed and shortened [*réduit et rapetissé*] according to the conformation given to it by the timbre, elaborates and fashions [*élabore et façonne*] the passages. The mouth is half opened. If one passes from the pianissimo to the mezzo-forte, one expends a little more air, but one maintains the action of the pharynx.

Finally, in the forte, it is necessary to support the passages with a vigorous pressure of the breath, a pressure which provokes a greater expenditure of the air. The pharynx then offers the tone a more spacious route, more developed in height or in width, according to the timbre; the movements of which we have just spoken are less flexible and less frequent, and the mouth, for its part, presents to the tone an easier outlet.

But agility itself is of two different natures: *di forza* (of power) and *di maniera* (of dexterity). These two natures are rarely found together in the same voice.

In the agility *di forza*, the passages are vigorously executed, especially the lively, powerful roulades, the dashing arpeggios. When this kind of passage ascends, one must necessarily fling it by means of a very sustained pressure of the air; this pressure increases with the strength and the rapidity of the passage; the pharynx, less mobile for the roulade and the arpeggio than for any other pattern, passes through the various degrees of fullness [*ampleur*] which the pitches and the strength of the tones require, maintaining the general form of the timbre. This agility has assumed the name of agility *di bravura* [bravery, or daring] because of the boldness, the strength, and the precision which characterize it.

In the agility *di maniera*, on the contrary, everything rests upon the skill of the singer. The contracted pharynx works slight and flexible movements such as the delicate and movable intonations of broken passages require. Here, a thin stream of air is sufficient. It is necessary, therefore, to not thrust [*lancer*] the passages, but to content oneself with nourishing the tones.

The agility *di maniera* never issues [*réussit*] as easily as the agility *di forza*; it is even necessary to hold it back a little in order to make its difficult intonations very distinct. One will have regard for this recommendation only in the pieces.

The inflections are obtained by allowing the throat the ease to dilate slightly with the impulse of each reinforced tone; the throat falls back into its original position for the following tone.

At half speed, most often the passages fail [*échappent*]; it is by supporting the tones, by distending the pharynx, and by flaunting [*étalant*], so to speak, the respiration that one remedies this fault.

From the principles which we have just set forth, it follows that it is much easier to vocalize *piano* than *forte*, that the same facility is obtained with the clear timbre rather than with the sombre timbre, for the first does not contract the pharynx at all. Open vowels are more favorable to fine agility than dark vowels.

Dotted notes and *syncopations*, materials of musical orthography, adhere more closely to the accents of the song than to vocalization. That is why we defer them to the second part. It is the same with the *tremolo*.

THE MANNER OF COMPOSING EXERCISES ☐

To the forms which we have indicated we would have been able to add a host of others, the number of the combinations extending to infinity. We advise the student to develop each pattern which troubles him by writing it out in keys in which he can sing it. This means will spare the voice many gropings.

One will have noticed that the exercises contained on pages 82-96, etc., are formed on the diatonic scale in the major mode by simply reproducing the passage which one has to study on each degree of the scale.

☐ When a pattern, other than those included in this work, is presented to the student, he will need to arrange it as we have done, by repeating the pattern on each degree of the diatonic scale, either in ascending or descending. If one wished, for example, to practice the passage: it would be necessary to write the

same pattern on each degree of the scale, however, without altering its
intervals.

EXAMPLE

There are some passages whose descending responses are presented awkwardly; one is forced either to vary them or to reverse them.

The passage  which forms the exercise:

EXAMPLE

should descend thus:

but the interval of the fourth being forced, we prefer to adopt the following form, substituting the interval of the third for that of the fifth:

*In the exercise:  we have

reversed the response [see exercise 222 on page 130].

*Other times the passage modulates as in the following example:

It is in the study of harmony that one will find the necessary help for developing similar passages. If a passage does not come off well later in the pieces, it will be necessary to detach it immediately from the phrase and arrange it into an exercise by one of the procedures which we have described. Otherwise, the student can even content himself with transposing it in its entirety by semitones. In that manner he makes the voice supple throughout its range and develops the flexibility of it in an equal manner.

In this first part we have presented to the student the primary elements of vocal instruction; we have traced for him the precepts which smoothe out for him the difficulties of performance. In the second part we will treat the application of all these resources to the different facets [*productions*] of the art.

END OF PART ONE

APPENDIX

APPENDIX I

VARIATIONS IN THE EDITION OF 1872

PRELIMINARY PAGES

$\boxed{A}$ The reader will probably have noticed that there is some
duplication of information in Garcia's prefatory material and in the
main text of his method. The 1872 edition does not include the reprint
of the *Mémoire*, as the 1841 edition does, but it includes much of the
same information as part of the main text, as well as the following
short chapter describing the vocal mechanism. This serves as chapter
one in the 1872 edition:

The mechanism of singing requires the cooperation of four distinct apparatuses acting simultaneously, but each fulfilling particular
functions, and with a complete independence from one another. These
apparatuses are:

1. The lungs   bellows

2. The larynx   vibrator

3. The pharynx   reflector

4. The organs of the mouth   articulators

Nature has superimposed these organs one on another. Essential
agents of respiration, the lungs are placed at the bottom of the instrument and fill the functions of an organ bellows which furnishes the air
which is necessary for the sonorous vibrations. The air enters the
lungs and exits from them through a multitude of little tubes called

bronchi, which, disposed in the manner of the branches of a tree, and by combining into a single tube which takes the name of trachea [*trachée-artère*] and rises vertically to the anterior portion of the neck.

This trachea, a slightly mobile and elastic [*extensible*] tube, is surmounted by the larynx, with which it connects.

The larynx, the producer *par excellence* of the voice, forms at the anterior part of the neck a protrusion which is noticeable to the view and to the touch, the Adam's apple. In its entirety it has, in a way, the form of a truncated cone whose base is reversed. Its cavity is very narrowed toward the middle, where it presents two horizontal membranes, one placed on the right, and the other on the left, and which are called vocal cords or *vocal tendons*.

The opening comprised between the tendons is named the glottis; that is why they also take the name of lips of the glottis. These lips alone have the property of giving birth to the vibrations. The form of the glottis is approximately triangular at the moment of inspiration, but it becomes elliptical as soon as one forms tones. We will see further on according to what principle the voice is produced and how the lips of the glottis function. Let us notice henceforth that they are not homogenous throughout their length; the posterior two fifths are formed by a cartilaginous prolongation, and the anterior three fifths by a tendon.

Above the vocal tendons are two long [*allongés*] recesses which are called the ventricles of the larynx, and which are each surmounted by a fold parallel to the vocal tendons. These folds leave between them a space which is the superior glottis, but which, much larger than the glottis properly so called, is never closed. Its function consists of encircling an elliptical space immediately above the inferior lips, narrowing or broadening it, and modifying in the most effective manner the volume and the timbre of the voice.

The superior opening of the larynx, free during the emission of the voice, is completely covered during the movements of deglutition by a sort of little tongue called the *epiglottis* which is situated behind the tongue.

The voice, on escaping from the glottis, reverberates above the larynx in the pharynx, a very elastic [*très extensible*] cavity which includes the space between the partition which one perceives at the back of the mouth upon lowering the tongue and the arch which forms the periphery of the throat. That cavity, by the numerous conformations which it can simulate, gives to the tones which the larynx produces the characteristics of the diverse timbres and the diverse vowels.

Finally, the tones pass through the mouth where some movable parts, the velum, the tongue, the lips, etc,, have the special function of giving the vowels their last degree of precision and of completing the word by articulating the consonants. But before considering the functions which the vocal organs fulfil, let us give a general sketch of the various kinds of sounds which the object of our studies makes.

[B] *The Different Kinds of Vocal Sounds* is the title of chapter two in the 1872 edition.

[C] The sentence following the symbol in the 1872 edition begins:

Experience demonstrates that, with the exception of the whistle, all the possible modifications of the tone, namely: the cry, the spoken voice, and the singing voice . . .

[D] Note that Garcia changed his opinion that the falsetto and head registers were a single register after his observations with the laryngoscope in 1854 and 1855. After that time, he considered the falsetto and head registers to be separate and distinct. The listing of the registers thus takes the following form in the sixth edition:

the chest;

the falsetto;

the head;

the contra-bass;

the inspiratory voice; . . .

[E] The sixth edition version of the line following the symbol follows:

And, finally, of the different characters of brilliance or of dullness [*sourdité*],[47]

and the different degrees of intensity and volume.

[F] At this point in the 1872 edition Garcia describes the first apparatus (the breathing mechanism), leading into it as follows:

Let us see now how these results proceed from the organs.

---

[47]Although one may say *voix sourde*, one has never said dullness [*sourdité*] of the voice. I ask pardon for using that new word, but it is necessary to explain a natural function of the glottis of which I believe myself the first to have become aware and described.

THE LUNGS--FIRST APPARATUS (Bellows)

The lungs are exclusively reservoirs where the air is accumulated, and not, as is rather generally thought, the place where tones
designated by the name of chest tones are developed.[48]

The lungs rest upon the diaphragm which separates them completely
from the abdomen and are moreover enveloped by the ribs. Their development, at the moment of inspiration, can be done at the same time both
vertically, by the contraction of the diaphragm, and laterally, by the
separation of the ribs.

If it were possible to isolate completely these two procedures,
which is at the least doubtful, which should be adopted as a preference
by the singer? Both, according to us, because from their cooperation
there results a complete respiration.

With women, the movements of respiration are operated more habitually by the lifting of the chest; would that not be caused by the dis-
comfort of the sides being habitually held?

[G] The 1872 presentation of the second apparatus begins:

THE LARYNX--SECOND APPARATUS (Vibrator)

The larynx, under the immediate dependence of the respiratory

---

[48]This error can be explained thus: men exclusively (who formed
the terminology), and women, if they speak or sing in the low part of
their voices, experience a strong vibration in the chest and in the
back; but, similar to the sounding board of a piano or violin, the chest
receives the vibrations by transmission and does not engender them.

apparatus, forms the registers, the various degrees of brilliance or of dullness of the tones, the intensity and the volume of the voice.

The Registers

By the word, register, we mean a series . . .

[H] The sentence preceding the symbol in the 1872 edition ends: . . . with which we will not concern ourselves.

[I] Garcia uses a different format for his discussion of the registers in the sixth edition. He discusses each register for both sexes before moving on to the next one. That version follows:

Chest Register

The chest register in the women's voices begins with one of the tones between e and a, according to the nature of the organ, and can reach as high as $c\#^2$ or d^2.

In the male voice this register, which is the principal one, includes a total scale of three octaves  from which each individual voice finds the range which is its own on the different points of that ladder. The ordinary limits of each voice are comprised between a twelfth and two octaves.

Falsetto Register

The falsetto register, for both sexes, begins at about g

and rises as far as c^2 or d^2.

One ascertains that in the female voice the falsetto register and the chest register have the same upper limit, and that they descend on the same tones as far as the tenth below, after which only the chest register continues to descend.

Head Register

The series of tones which follows when rising from the falsetto register takes the name of head voice.

The head voice in men, just as real as in women, is a remnant of the child's voice and is only a weak resource for them.

In Italy the public places no value on it. The head tones, properly so called, can be used only in exceptional cases by some very high tenors; all other singers, with the exception of the *buffi caricati*, would be wrong to make use of it.

[The summary of the registers is identical in the sixth edition and in the *Mémoire*, with the exception of the sections indicated with asterisks in the *Mémoire*.]

[J] In the sixth edition the passage on the timbres begins:

THE PHARYNX--THIRD APPARATUS (Reflector)

The pharynx is the apparatus which modifies the tone with regard to the timbres.

Just as the voice is submitted to the distinction of the registers, so is it also inevitably to the difference of the timbres.

K̲ Instead of the sentence preceding this symbol, the 1872 edition has the following two sentences:

The variety of the timbres results first from the various systems
of vibration which the larynx contains, then from the modifications
imparted to the tones by the pharynx. We will study here the timbres
produced by the pharynx.

L̲ In the sentence following the symbol the sixth edition reads:
. . . those of the form, the volume, the consistency, . . .

M̲ The 1872 edition uses the word "volume" [*ampleur*] instead of
"penetration" [*mordant*] in the sentence following the symbol.

N̲ The reader is urged to compare the five paragraphs preceding
this symbol with the final six paragraphs in the chapter entitled *The
Formation of Tones* (chapter III-A).

O̲ Compare the paragraph preceding the symbol with the third
paragraph under the heading, *The Formation of the Timbres*, in chapter
III-A, *The Formation of Tones*.

P̲ The sentence preceding the symbol is replaced in the 1872
edition by the following two sentences:

Numerous defects can alter the beauty of the voice. We are going
to make known the most habitual and indicate the means of correcting
them.

Q̲ The presentation of the *Gutteral Timbre* is slightly different in the 1872 edition. That version follows:

When the tongue broadens at the base, it presses the epiglottis
back onto the column of air, and the voice comes out as though squashed.
One can verify this disposition of the tongue by pressing exteriorly a
little above the larynx with the fingers. The tone, even under the
pressure of the fingers, would not take a guttural timbre if the tongue
were not swollen at the base.

One sees easily what one must do to correct the defectiveness of
this timbre: the tongue, which is principally charged, by its movements,
with transforming the voice into vowels, will need to be moved, especially by its lateral edges, slightly [*faiblement*] by the middle, and
not at all by the base. Let us add that the separation of the jaws
should be approximately uniform for all the vowels.

R̄ The first sentence of the section on the *Nasal Timbre* in the
sixth edition reads:

When the velum is too relaxed, the voice can receive a nasal timbre, for the column of sonorous air goes directly to take its reverbera-
tion in the nasal fossae before flowing out through the mouth.

S̄ The sentence preceding the symbol is replaced in the 1872
edition by the following sentence: It is sufficient to lift the velum
to correct this defect.

T̄ Compare the section on *Intensity and Volume* in the *Memoire*
with that given in the sixth edition in chapter III-A.

CHAPTER I

[A] The 1872 edition devotes its fourth chapter (a short one) to the subject of *Aptitudes of the Student.*

[B] Chapter four of the 1872 edition begins:

The most favorable conditions, after that of intelligence, are a true passion for music, the aptitude to grasp quickly . . .

[C] The final paragraph of chapter four in the 1872 edition begins:

Singers, so strongly interested in preserving their instruments, the most delicate and fragile of all, will understand . . .

[D] The paragraph following this symbol is the penultimate one in chapter four of the sixth edition.

[E] Chapter eight in the sixth edition is entitled *Some Observations on the Manner of Studying the Exercises.*

[F] The two sentences preceding this symbol were reversed in the 1872 edition. The first and third paragraphs following the symbol are the opening ones of chapter eight in the 1872 edition. The gist of the third paragraph of chapter eight of the sixth edition appears as the first complete paragraph on page nine. The translator has used his editorial judgement to place them in the present order.

[G] The corresponding paragraph in the 1841 edition reads:

Once the first difficulties are overcome one will practice on the seven Italian vowels: [a], [e], [ɛ], [i], [o], [ɔ], [u], and preferably on the vowels [a], [e], [ɛ], [o], [ɔ].

[H] The paragraph in chapter eight of the 1872 edition which corresponds to the one preceding the symbol reads:

The exercises which follow will often present the passage from the chest register to that of the falsetto and *vice versa*. Far from avoiding that passage, it will be necessary to make it heard boldly as often as it occurs in the exercise. Time and patience will make the separation, at first shocking, disappear.

CHAPTER II

[A] This subject is treated in chapter five of the sixth edition.

[B] The corresponding section in the sixth edition is concerned with the falsetto register as applied to all women's voices. The range examples presented at the bottom of page sixteen and in the first paragraph below are from the sixth edition. The corresponding ranges given in the 1841 edition are  and respectively. The 1872 version follows:

In all the women's voices this [falsetto] register is approximately identical in its range, different in its intensity and beauty. It forms the noteworthy [*remarquable*] part of the mezzo-soprano voice. The mezzo-soprano voices can become equal and full throughout their range by the use of the three registers. This kind of voice has great resources for musical coloring. The falsetto register descends almost as low as the chest and rises as high , but the portion  is generally so weak that it cannot be sustained with the same degree of intensity as the corresponding range of the chest register, nor render the effect of any sentiment with even a little energy.

One sees by what precedes that although the chest and falsetto registers can traverse the same tones of the scale, it is not unimportant which register is chosen. First, the character of the sonority of the one is, as it were, the opposite of the other. The chest register is vigorous and penetrating and is suitable to warm and energetic emotions; the falsetto register is covered and soft and renders better the sweet sentiments or one of contained sadness. But, independently of these considerations, here is what should above all, in our opinion, guide women singers in the use of the registers:

The tones  in the chest register require, in the proportion that one seeks to attain them, such an expenditure of effort that two or three years of practice would be enough to change the organ in a disastrous and irremediable manner. These same tones in the falsetto register are, on the contrary, easy to use and without disadvantages. Thus, in order to avoid both the weakness of the low tones of the falsetto register and also the efforts which the high tones of the chest register require, the series of tones which concerns us should be formed by the joining of the two registers:

Chest Falsetto

from ⚬ to ⚬⚬⚬ from ⚬⚬⚬ to ⚬

We maintain four tones common to the two registers in order to facilitate the passage from the one register to the other.

CHAPTER III-B

A̅ The timbres are discussed in Part One of the 1872 edition as parts of chapter two, *The Various Kinds of Vocal Sounds*, and chapter three, *The Formation of Tones* (see chapter III-A). Also see pages I-lxiii in the preliminary pages.

B̅ The paragraph preceding the symbol appears in chapter six, *The Emission and Qualities of the Voice*, in the 1872 edition.

CHAPTER IV

A̅ *Breathing* is a subheading in chapter six, *The Emission and Qualities of the Voice*, in the sixth edition.

B̅ The references to "two movements" in the sentence preceding this symbol and to the "double procedure" in the paragraph following the symbol are confusing, since we have a total of *three* movements after collating the editions. The 1872 instruction to "lower the diaphragm," it could be argued, is merely a refinement of the 1841 advice to "set the hollow of the stomach," but there seemed to be sufficient difference for us to decide that both forms should be presented.

C̅ The two paragraphs preceding this symbol are replaced in the 1872 edition by a single paragraph placed between the first and second paragraphs of the section on *Breathing*. It reads:

The lungs, in order to receive exterior air, need for the walls

of the chest to separate to provide for them a space where they can
dilate freely. To this increase in capacity is added that of the lowering of the diaphragm, a broad and convex muscle arising from the sides
of the chest, which, while serving as the base of the chest, separates
it from the abdomen.

CHAPTER V

[A] *The Emission and the Qualities of the Voice* is the title of
chapter six in the 1872 edition.

[B] The reader is urged to compare the section following the
symbol with the similar one in the *Mémoire* on pages lx-lxiii. Note
that, in addition to the defective timbres, the *Mémoire* describes one
acceptable one, the *Round Timbre*. Where there are slight differences in
wording between the 1841 and 1872 editions, we have chosen to use that
of the 1872 version.

[C] In the *Mémoire* the hollow timbre is called the harsh [*rauque*]
timbre.

[D] The wording for the section on the position of the mouth is
abridged in the sixth edition as follows:

According to common opinion, the more the mouth is opened the
easier and the more powerful is the emission of the voice; one can
affirm the complete opposite. An excessive separation of the jaws has
the effect of constricting the pharynx, and, as a consequence, extin-
guishes the voice by removing its vault-like resonance chamber. This
exaggerated opening of the mouth is not the only defect from which the

singer must protect himself: (1) if the teeth are closed too tightly, the voice contracts a guttural character; (2) if one advances the lips in the form of a funnel, one obtains only dull, barking tones; (3) if one opens the mouth in an oval (like a fish), that position has the disadvantage of dulling the tone, of mixing the vowels into each other, of impeding the articulation, and finally, of giving the face a hard and ungraceful [*disgracieuse*] expression.

[E] The paragraph preceding this symbol is from the 1872 edition. A comparable paragraph appears in chapter three of the 1841 edition as the second paragraph on the clear timbre. That paragraph follows:

Beyond the $f\#^1$, this timbre becomes disagreeable, and whatever the ability of the singer, man or woman, the tones g^1 through b^1 seem shrill and recall the voices of choir boys, even when they are heard in a huge building.

[F] In the sixth edition the *General Table for the Emission of Tones* appears at the beginning of chapter nine, *Vocalization Exercises*.

CHAPTER VI

[A] The subject of *Blending the Registers* is a subheading in the chapter on *The Emission and Qualities of the Voice* in the sixth edition.

[B] In the 1872 edition the exercises for blending the chest and falsetto registers appear with all the other exercises in chapter nine, *Vocalization Exercises*.

CHAPTER VII

[A] This passage is rendered in the sixth edition as follows:

Thus, to vocalize will mean, for us, the ability to connect the tones to each other freely.

There are five ways of connecting the tones of any passage:

One may carry [*porte*] them;

One may tie [*lie*] them;

One may mark them;

One may detach [*pique*] them;

One may aspirate them (a rare manner).

[B] The paragraph preceding the symbol was placed at the end of chapter seven, *Vocalization*, in the sixth edition. Garcia used all of that chapter to discuss the five means of articulation mentioned in note [A] above.

[C] The ending of the sentence preceding this symbol reads as follows in the 1872 version: " . . . which make the performance tremulous, indistinct, or gliding [*tremblante, cotoneuse, glissée*]."

The French word in the 1841 edition which we translated as "indistinct" was "*confuse*"; the translator of the Oliver Ditson edition of Part One translated the French word "*cotoneuse*" as "indistinct."

[D] The two sentences preceding this symbol were changed in the 1872 version as follows: One will succeed in it by adding to each note an impulse of air, produced by a pressure of the stomach and a dilation of the pharynx. That dilation should produce the effect of the same

220

vowel repeated as many times as there are notes in the passage.

[E] The 1841 version of the sentence preceding the symbol reads: This fault slows the tempo of the scales; it is preferable to make the impetus [*élan*] clear right from the first note.

[F] The sentence between the asterisks is replaced in the sixth edition by the following two sentences: Each tone is surrounded by four appoggiaturas, two above and two below; those above, like those below, are one at a distance of a whole tone from the given tone, the other at a distance of a semitone. In the modern style the appoggiatura rising from the distance of a whole tone is the least used; here is an example which combines the other three kinds:

**Mozart: *Clemenza di Tito*

[G] The version of this exercise given in the 1872 edition seemed more in accord with the advice given in the second paragraph on page 163; consequently, that version was included in the main text rather than the higher version from the 1841 edition. That 1841 version follows:

[H] In the sixth edition Garcia presents the exercises for *Little Notes* after his presentation of the *Mordents* and before that of the *Trill*.

[I] *The Manner of Composing Exercises* was presented (without a subject heading) at the end of chapter eight, *Some Observations on the Manner of Studying the Exercises*, of the sixth edition.

[J] The 1872 version of this paragraph begins: When a form must be developed, the student will arrange it . . . .